Acknowledgments

The authors gratefully acknowledge the financial support and sponsorship of the College Board.

Preliminary reports of this study's findings were presented at the National Forum of the College Board (New York, October 1984) and at the Middle States Regional Meeting of the College Board (Washington, February 1985). Study findings were also presented at two day-long workshops held in connection with the New England and Midwest Regional Meetings of the College Board. These "Financial Aid and Enrollment Marketing" workshops were held in Newton, Massachusetts and in Chicago in February 1986. The comments of the participants at these meetings and workshops were helpful in shaping the final study report and in suggesting a number of useful additional analyses.

The authors wish to express their particular appreciation to James Nelson of the College Board for his early participation in study planning and his continuing encouragement throughout the project. They also wish to acknowledge the contribution of D. Edwin Lebby and Caroline Cuthbert of Annapolis Research and Communications Associates in conducting the telephone interviewing for with this project. Shannon Gangl provided helpful research and computing assistance in the early stages of the data-analysis phase.

The authors assume full responsibility for the contents of this report and for any remaining errors. The authors are listed in alphabetical order.

College Choices of Academically Able Students

The Influence of No-Need Financial Aid and Other Factors

Research Monograph No. 10

by Randall G. Chapman
University of Alberta

Rex Jackson
Applied Educational Research, Inc.

College Entrance Examination Board, New York, 1987

Authors are encouraged to express freely their professional judgment. Therefore, points of view or opinions stated in College Board books do not necessarily represent official College Board position or policy.

Inquiries regarding this publication should be addressed to Editorial Office, The College Board, 45 Columbus Avenue, New York, New York 10023-6917.

Copies of this publication may be ordered from College Board Publications, Box 886, New York, New York 10101. The price is $12.95.

Cover photograph by Glenn Foss.

Library of Congress Catalog Card Number: 86-073023

ISBN: 0-87447-2792

Printed in the United States of America.

9 8 7 6 5 4 3 2 1

Contents

1. Introduction and summary of principal findings

This chapter describes the purpose of the study and the organization of the report, and it provides a description of the research design and a summary of the main study findings.

Our conclusions are based on a large-scale survey research study, sponsored by the College Board, concerned with the college preferences and choices of a sample of high-ability high school seniors applying to colleges in the spring of 1984. The main objective of this research effort was to assess the degree to which high school students with high academic ability are currently being awarded aid on a no-need (or "merit") basis and the degree to which such financial aid influences college choices, in relation to other factors.

Study background and context

Several concerns prompted the initiation of this study. Surveys of institutions concerning their financial aid policies suggest that the number of colleges awarding some aid on a no-need or academic basis, without regard to financial need considerations, is growing. Several surveys in the mid-to-late 1970s (Huff 1975; Sidar and Potter 1978: the College Board/AACRAO 1980) provided estimates that about 55 to 65 percent of four-year colleges and universities used no-need criteria in making financial aid awards. More recently, in a survey conducted by the College Board and the National Association of Student Financial Aid Administrators (NASFAA) in 1984, 85 percent of four-year private colleges responding to the survey and 90 percent of four-year public colleges stated that they offered some awards on an academic basis without regard to financial need considerations.

For colleges responding to the 1984 College Board/NASFAA survey, the average no-need award was $835 for public institutions (with 80 percent of the awards under $1,000) and $1,558 for private institutions (with 51 percent under $1,000). However, some awards are appreciably larger than these figures suggest. For example, private colleges reported that 20 percent of their no-need aid awards exceeded $2,000, and 6 percent exceeded $4,000.

Many colleges have always had some scholarships for which financial need has not been a relevant consideration in the awarding decision. However, the use of financial aid as an enrollment inducement has apparently become increasingly widespread in recent years. In the College Board/ NASFAA survey, about 36 percent of the public and 51 percent of the private colleges stated that no-need awards were used *primarily* as a recruitment device, in contrast to a means for recognizing outstanding achievement. In another recent survey (Porter and McColloch 1982), 80 percent of colleges awarding no-need aid reported that such aid was used either to "a great extent" or to "some extent" in recruiting. It seems clear, therefore, that attracting academically able students to the campus is at least one of the motives underlying many institutions' use of no-need financial aid awards.

Study focus and approach

From a research perspective, the relevant issues become those of determining the real impact of no-need awards on the college choices of the high-ability students who are the target of such scholarships. Presuming that these awards do influence students' college choices in a material fashion, some policy analysis inquiries naturally follow. Of particular concern would be how colleges might compete for high-ability students in other ways than just resorting to no-need scholarships of their own. This involves identifying and quantifying the role of other, nonmonetary factors in the college choice decision-making process. Cost–benefit analyses are relevant here, too. What is the cost of using no-need scholarships? Are there other more cost-effective ways to attract high-ability students?

Since the focus of this study is on no-need financial aid awarded on the basis of academic criteria, the relevant study population is high-ability high school students. These are the students who will attract the no-need awards, since the purpose of such awards increasingly appears to be to encourage particularly desirable students to enroll at a college. Here, "desirable" is presumed to be defined in the usual academic terms. To many colleges, it may include other considerations as well, including those of athletic ability or leadership skills and potential. This study is principally concerned, however, with the influence of financial aid on college choice and with the use of academic criteria by colleges in making aid awards.

Organization of the report

This report is organized into three main parts describing our approach to the research problem, our findings on the main research questions related to the determinants of college choice behavior of high-ability students, and findings on auxiliary issues associated with the college choice process.

The first part of this report provides a description of the theoretical framework for this research and a discussion of a number of methodological and measurement issues associated with studying college choice behavior (Chapter 2).

The second part describes the study of college choice and financial aid awarding behavior, including: a description of the study design and associated data collection procedures (Chapter 3); presentation and discussion of empirical findings with respect to the role of college costs and financial aid in relation to other factors in determining high-ability students' college choices (Chapter 4); and presentation and discussion of empirical findings with respect to determinants of colleges' financial aid awards (Chapter 5).

The final section provides descriptions of empirical findings on other aspects of college choice behavior, including: antecedents of choice behavior, including preference judgment formation (Chapter 6) and perception judgment formation (Chapter 7); other influences on choice behavior, including college campus visits and post-admissions contacts (Chapter 8); and changes in college plans after initial decisions—actual fall enrollment compared to choices reported in the spring (Chapter 9).

The theoretical framework

To assess the role of no-need awards on the college choices of high-ability high school students, we have constructed a general model of college choice behavior. The fundamental premise underlying this research effort is that the role of financial aid in general—and no-need awards in particular—as a determining factor in college choice may be assessed only within the context of all the other factors at work when students choose colleges. It is impossible to assess the role of any single factor in a complex decision process like college choice except relative to other considerations.

The major support for this premise comes from past studies of the college choice process, such as those of Radner and Miller (1975), Kohn, Manski, and Mundel (1976), Chapman (1979), and Manski and Wise (1983). These studies demonstrate that college quality, reputation, and prestige appear to be the most important considerations in the college choice process. Financial considerations certainly exist, but they seem to be of secondary importance. Nonetheless, the key question is still how important the monetary considerations are relative to other factors. The current study was designed specifically to gather the most extensive data to date on financial aid in general, and no-need financial aid awards in particular, in order to address this issue of the relative importance of financial aid.

Our multistage model of college choice behavior consists of three major components: perception formation, preference judgment formation, and choice. We seek to explain the determinants of how students perceive colleges (what objectively verifiable college attributes are related to students' perceptions), how these perceptions are implicitly combined and weighed to form an overall summary measure of the "value" of a particular college to a student (prior preference), and ultimately how prior preference and other factors (such as monetary considerations) lead to actual observed college choices. Because of our particular concern with the influence of financial aid

on students' college choices, we have studied and analyzed the final phases (preference and choice) in the greatest detail. Chapter 2 describes the multistage model of college choice behavior used throughout this study as a framework for study design, data organization, and analysis.

Study design and data collection

Most studies of college choice, such as institutional "yield rate" studies, collect data for samples of students who have all been admitted to a given institution. In such admitted applicant studies, information is gathered only after final choices are made. In contrast, this study is based on a national probability sample of 2,000 high-ability high school seniors who had taken the College Board's Scholastic Aptitude Test (SAT). Students in the sample were contacted twice, before and after the actual college choice decision.

The sample of students was first surveyed in March 1984 by means of a mail questionnaire. Information was sought with regard to the colleges to which students had applied, their current rankings of the top three colleges in order of preference, self-reported importance weights for factors in college choice, and their ratings of the top three colleges based on these factors.

Those students who had responded to the first survey and who had reported applying to more than one college were contacted again by telephone in May–June 1984. Information gathered during this second phase included the status of admissions offers received, specific financial aid offers made by those colleges offering admission, and the final choice of college to attend.

Thus, within this multistage study design, we are able to analyze the preferences stated by students at a time *before* aid offers from most colleges were known, the actual aid offers *later* received, and *final* choices. As a consequence, we are able to isolate the effects of aid offers and to assess their influence on choices after taking into account prior preferences.

A total of 1,549 responses to the mail survey were obtained, representing a response rate of 77.5 percent. Of these respondents, 325 reported that they had applied to (and in virtually all cases been accepted by) a single college. Of the remaining 1,224 students who had applied to at least two colleges, 1,183 were eventually contacted by telephone, for a response rate to the telephone survey of 96.7 percent.

Chapter 3 describes the study-design and data-collection methodology in detail.

Determinants of choice behavior

Chapter 4 contains a complete description of the study findings with regard to the determinants of college choice behavior. Here, a brief overview is provided.

Preliminary remarks

Given our two-stage research design, it was possible to separate a student's prior preference for a college from his actual choice behavior. Prior preference is unconstrained by whether the student was admitted to a college but also—most important—it is designed to be independent of monetary considerations. Monetary considerations, and other situational constraints, are factored back in the choice equation in the actual choice phase.

It is important to note that we are studying college choice behavior, *not* college search behavior. Our study begins at the point where students have formed their application sets, the colleges to which they have submitted applications. We must presume that all such colleges are minimally satisfactory on all major dimensions of choice or else would have been excluded from the application set. However, since students do not know their exact out-of-pocket costs until they receive financial aid offers, costs may act also as a constraint on final choices, making the selection of some college options infeasible.

Major results

About 61 percent of our students with choice sets of two or more actually chose to attend their original highest-preference college (to which they were admitted). The remaining 39 percent switched from their original highest-preference college to another college. We need to examine the forces which led some students to follow through with their original preferences while others switched. Those who switched mentioned the following major factors as being influential: better financial aid (27.4 percent), lower costs (23.1 percent), campus visits (12.6 percent), location (11.9 percent), and academic reputation (11.9 percent). Thus, over half these students reported money as a factor in their switching. (In interpreting these findings, it is important to note that direct self-reports for those students who remained loyal to their original first-choice college were not collected, so comparisons between those who switched and those who remained loyal is not possible.)

While these self-reported reasons for changes in choice are of general interest, it is important to note that such self-reports are subject to a variety of possible distortions. In general, inferences drawn from actual choice behavior and the objective correlates of that behavior are more likely to be dependable. For this reason, the main focus of our analysis is on the development and estimation of a statistical model of college choice behavior. This model provides estimates of the relative importance of a number of factors in influencing college choices. Most important, the statistical model used—the multinomial logit model—provides quantitative estimates of college choice determinants, thus making it possible to assess, for example, how much choice probabilities change in response to changes in financial aid.

Our results indicate that prior preference for a college is the primary and paramount determinant of college choice behavior. Operationally, prior preference was assessed by means of the rankings of the top three colleges provided by students in the first-stage survey. These earlier preferences dominate all other factors in the choice of a college. Other statistically meaningful determinants of college choice do exist, but prior preference is the predominant indicator of which college a student will ultimately choose.

Monetary considerations have a smaller but statistically detectable influence on college choice. Other things being equal, total college costs detract from a college's attractiveness, while scholarship aid adds to its desirability. Other non-grant components of financial aid, such as loans and part-time jobs, appear to have no influence on college choice behavior.

The relatively modest role played by monetary considerations might well have been expected in the context of a study of college choice. Colleges which were perceived to be too expensive (even taking into account expected financial aid) may have been ruled out of consideration during the college search phrase, prior to the formation of an application set. Also, this finding is in accord with the empirical results of previous studies of college choice behavior: college quality is the primary determinant of college choice, with financial considerations being of secondary importance.

Another factor influencing college choice behavior is the student's perceived chance of having a financial aid offer renewed: greater perceived renewability is positively related to choice. Students seem to implicitly discount scholarship aid that is only offered on a one-time basis, with little or no chance of being renewed. The magnitude of this implicit discounting is substantial—so much so that colleges should probably not even offer such nonrenewable aid.

Students appear to prefer colleges whose academic level (as measured by SAT scores) is comparable to their own. Thus, an "academic quality zoning" hypothesis is supported by our results: students prefer colleges that enroll students with academic abilities like their own.

A number of other potential influencers and moderators of choice behavior were examined: (a) whether a student's father or mother attended a college; (b) the distance from a college's campus to a student's residence; (c) portable financial aid from state and private scholarship programs; and (d) whether a student had applied for financial aid but had not been offered it by a college. None of these factors had any statistically significant influence on college choice behavior, given the presence of the other variables (described above) in the model. Of course, certain of these variables may have been influential when students formed their application sets. However, after the application set formation decision, these variables appear to have no material influence on the ultimate college choice behavior of high-ability high school seniors.

Implications of the results

The statistical modeling approach employed in this study yields estimated relative importance weights which measure the implicit trade-offs high-ability students make when they choose among various colleges to which they have been admitted. Thus, for example, it is possible to estimate the amount of scholarship aid that would approximately offset a college being a second-choice rather than a first-choice alternative, on a prior preference basis. It is also possible to estimate the implicit discounting that high-ability students attach to aid which is perceived to be nonrenewable. In addition, it is possible to construct elaborate and realistic choice scenarios and to use the relative importance weights in combination with the statistical model of choice (the multinomial logit model) to predict the likelihood of students choosing certain colleges under specified choice situations.

Chapter 4 describes the detailed empirical findings with regard to the determinants of college choice behavior. A number of sample scenarios and trade-off situations, similar to those described below, are used to illustrate this study's findings regarding the factors at work when high-ability students make college choice decisions. Additional cost–benefit analyses regarding the use of scholarship aid are examined in Chapter 4.

The influence of scholarship aid on choice. The influence of scholarships on college choice behavior can be illustrated by considering a student who is "indifferent" between two college alternatives. That is, considering all factors—including prior preference, college costs, financial aid, perceived renewability of the aid, and the academic "fit" of the student at the colleges (in terms of SAT scores)—our hypothetical high-ability student equally prefers two colleges. The probability of such a student choosing each college would be 50 percent. Alternatively, 100 such students who, on average, are indifferent between two college alternatives would be expected to ultimately split their choices 50–50 between the two colleges.

Now, suppose that one of the colleges offers an additional amount of scholarship aid, either in the form of a no-need aid award or by enriching the existing financial aid package to have a greater component of grant (as compared to loans and part-time jobs). Our statistical model shows predictions (Table 1.1) of the student's revised choice probabilities, depending on the amount of aid offered.

Table 1.1 suggests that scholarship aid will influence high-ability students to some extent. However, substantial amounts of aid are required to affect choice materially. It should be noted that this illustration applies only to a specific hypothetical situation: that of a student who is facing a choice between two colleges and is not predisposed toward either (both colleges are equally preferred). Different assumptions about the choice situation will, of course, lead to different

Table 1.1. Illustrative probabilities and effective costs

Amount of extra grant	Revised probability of choosing the college offering the extra grant (%)	Effective scholarship cost per student
$ 0	50.0	$ 0
$1,000	57.2	$ 7,944
$2,000	64.1	$ 9,092
$3,000	70.5	$10,317
$4,000	76.2	$11,634
$5,000	81.1	$13,039

results. Several more complex and realistic situations are illustrated below and in Chapter 4.

Note that in Table 1.1 the effective scholarship cost per additional student per year to the college is considerably above the actual scholarship value. This occurs because some of the students with 50–50 choice probabilities would have enrolled without such scholarships. (This situation, and the definition and calculation of effective costs, is discussed further in Chapter 4.)

Scholarship aid, prior preference, and choice. Another way to illustrate the impact of scholarships on college choice behavior is by considering how much extra scholarship aid would be required to offset the disadvantage of not being the original first-choice prior preference college. Consider a hypothetical student with two colleges in his or her choice set which are similar on all factors except for original first-choice prior preference. In such a case, our results imply that, on average, the original first-preference college would be chosen by the student about 80 percent of the time. Our results predict that the original second-choice college would have to offer an additional scholarship of about $4,700 to improve its chances of choice to 50 percent (from 20 percent).

This result illustrates the primacy of prior preference over money: prior preference is extremely important to high-ability students, and monetary considerations are secondary in influence. In effect, high-ability students tend to choose the college that they view most highly, almost regardless of the financial consequences. However, a relatively large amount of scholarship aid has, as might be expected, some influence on the college choices of these students.

An illustration of choice between private and public colleges. A typical scenario involving the use of no-need aid is for a high-cost private college to offer such financial support to compete more favorably with a low-cost public institution. Of course, other considerations (such as perceived relative college quality) may operate in favor of the private college. Our results shed light on the costs associated with such no-need aid award actions on the part of the (relatively) high-cost private college. The use of no-need scholarship aid will improve the likelihood of the student choosing the no-need, aid-awarding college. However, the key issue concerns how sensitive the choice probabilities are to no-need aid and also, from the college's perspective, the expected cost of pursuing such a policy.

To investigate the economics of awarding such no-need aid, we will *assume that the student in question is from a high-income family* (in which case no-need aid is the only kind of financial aid that could be offered). This high-income assumption is important. As discussed in Chapter 4, there are some differences in the implicit relative-importance weights used by students in various income strata. See Chapter 4 for details on these differences.

The following additional assumptions are made in this scenario:

	College A (private)	College B (public)
Total costs	$12,000	$5,000
Grant aid offered	To be determined	None
Renewal of grant aid?	Is guaranteed	Not relevant
SATFIT	100	150

SATFIT is the difference (in absolute value) between the student's SAT score and the average SAT scores of all students at a college. All other considerations not mentioned above are assumed to be equal for both colleges (except when modified in the following discussion and analysis).

In this situation, our statistical model predicts that the base choice probability when college A offers $0 of no-need aid is 42.8 percent (assuming that colleges A and B are equally preferred on a prior-preference basis). The substantial disadvantage that college A faces with much higher costs is only partially offset by a better SATFIT (100 versus 150).

Some alternative situations involving various amounts of no-need scholarship aid (from $0 to $5,000) and various prior preference situations are displayed in Table 1.2.

The last case described in Table 1.2—when the no-need aid awarding college is not the original first-choice prior preference college—is particularly noteworthy. The private college that uses no-need aid to compete with an otherwise preferred (on a prior preference basis) public college can increase its choice probability from 13.3 to 54.3 percent by offering $5,000 of no-need aid. As in other examples described here and in Chapter 4, it appears that relatively large amounts of money are required to induce substantial changes in choice probabilities.

Additional implicit trade-offs and choice scenarios. Chapter 4 contains extensive discussion of the implicit trade-offs made by high ability students in their college choice decision making. Also, other choice scenarios are examined to illustrate the application of the empirical findings.

Determinants of financial aid awards

The 1,183 students with whom interviews were completed in this study received a total of 3,988 admissions offers. Of the 1,183 students, 754 (64

Table 1.2. Illustrative probabilities

| | Probability of choosing college A, if college A offers the following amounts of no-need scholarship aid | | | | | |
	$0	$1,000	$2,000	$3,000	$4,000	$5,000
If colleges A and B are equally preferred on a prior preference basis	42.8	53.2	63.0	71.9	79.3	85.2
If college A is the first-choice prior preference college	78.4	84.6	89.2	92.5	94.9	96.5
If college A is the second-choice prior preference college	13.3	19.0	26.0	34.5	44.2	54.3

percent) received at least one offer of financial aid. Of the 3,988 admission offers, 1,486 (37 percent) were accompanied by an offer of financial aid. The extent to which these financial aid offers were based on academic considerations can be estimated in several ways.

Students offered financial aid were asked during telephone interviews whether any of the offers they received were based in whole or in part on academic considerations. A total of 572 of these high-ability students (48 percent of the sample and 76 percent of those offered any aid) indicated having received aid offers based at least in part on academic criteria. Use of no-need criteria was also evident in the number of aid offers to students who had not applied for aid. Of the 3,988 admissions offers, 1,659 were to students who had not applied for aid at the college offering admission. About 14 percent of these 1,659 non-aid applicants actually received financial aid offers from colleges.

Data available for individuals in the sample (including measures of family financial circumstances and academic ability), as well as data available for colleges offering admission and aid to these students, permitted development of statistical models to account for the incidence and amounts of aid awards in terms of both individual and institutional factors. Several main conclusions were supported by these analyses.

With regard to the incidence of financial aid awards to students who applied for aid:
▪ Incidence of aid awards (the probability that a student will be offered any aid) was determined primarily by financial need (college costs in relation to expected family contribution) for students offered admission at colleges ranking highest on a proxy measure of academic reputation.
▪ Academic ability played a stronger role than financial need in determining whether or not aid applicants would be offered any aid by colleges ranking below the top 80 colleges on the measure of academic reputation.

With regard to the incidence of financial aid awards to students who did not apply for aid:
▪ Students reported receiving aid offers for which they had not applied from colleges with high ranks on the reputation measure as well as from those with lower ranks. However, such offers were made far more often by lower-ranking than by higher-ranking colleges.
▪ For both high- and low-ranking colleges, academic ability as measured by SAT scores was strongly associated with offers of aid to students not applying for it.

With regard to amounts of aid:

• Over 20 percent of aid offers reported by students exceeded "need," defined here as the difference between total college costs and expected family contribution calculated by the College Board's College Scholarship Service. There are a number of reasons why aid awards may exceed "need" calculated in this way, since institutions use a larger body of information about applicants in determining aid awards. We found, however, that for both high- and low-ranking groups of colleges on the academic reputation measure, the chances of a student receiving an aid offer exceeding need (as defined above) increased markedly with increasing SAT scores. Thus, the amount of aid awards appears to be, in part, a function of students' standing with respect to academic criteria.

It should be noted that in the analyses leading to the above conclusions, colleges were grouped on an academic reputation measure. Thus, these conclusions apply in an aggregate sense to colleges belonging to different groups. Individual colleges may well have financial aid policies and practices different from those characteristic of their groups, and thus these conclusions cannot be assumed to apply to any given institution.

In sum, the results of our analyses of aid offers appear to be highly consistent with other information on allocation of discretionary aid by institutions. Colleges in our highest-ranking group on an index of academic quality (ones which also attracted a highly disproportionate share of applications from students in our sample) appear to be more responsive to need than to academic "merit" in determining whether to offer financial aid to admitted high-ability students. Colleges ranking lower on our academic quality index (ones that are at a disadvantage in competing for able students) appear to be offering no-need aid with greater frequency to able students. While these differences among college groups were evident from our data, it was also apparent that at least some of the higher-ranking colleges were responding to academic criteria in determining amounts of aid awards and in offering aid to students not applying for it.

Chapter 5 describes in detail the empirical findings with regard to financial aid incidence and determinants.

Antecedents of choice behavior: Preference and perception formation

Given the paramount importance of prior preference in college choice decision-making behavior, the natural question arises as to the determinants of prior preference. Our results indicate that perceived college academic quality is the main determinant of prior preferences for colleges. In turn, the main influencer of perceived college quality is actual college quality, as proxied by an index formed from a number of objectively verifiable college quality measures.

Prior preference for a college is principally influenced by a student's perceptions of the college's academic quality. Our composite academic quality perception index included such underlying perception rating scales as "academic facilities," "overall academic reputation," "availability of special majors, degrees, or honors programs," "preparation for career or graduate and professional school opportunities," and "academic strength in your major areas of interest." A student's perceptions of a college's lifestyle, quality of personal contact, and location are secondary—but important—factors involved in the college preference judgment formation process.

Actual college quality is the primary determinant of students' perceptions of academic quality. Other interpretable and statistically significant linkages exist between a college's objectively verifiable characteristics and students' perceptions of academic quality, lifestyle, quality of personal contact, and location. These linkages are described in Chapter 7.

Chapters 6 and 7 describe in detail the empirical findings with regard to the determinants of the antecedents of choice behavior—preference judgment formation and perception formation.

Other factors influencing college choice behavior

The role, incidence, and influence of campus visits and post-admissions contacts are analyzed in Chapter 8. Main findings include a high correspondence between campus visits and student choice behavior, the infrequent incidence of post-admissions contacts of any kind, and the generally positive impact of all kinds of post-admissions contacts. The source of the contact (e.g., admissions representative versus faculty member) does not seem to matter: all contacts are generally viewed as being either positive or neutral, with very few contacts being reported as negatively influencing students' views of colleges. These results suggest that careful and thoughtful management of such post-admissions contact activities is desirable.

Changes in college plans after initial decisions

A follow-up survey of our sample in the fall of 1984 found that 98 percent of respondents enrolled in the colleges they indicated as their original choices in an earlier survey stage. For students applying to only one college, earlier choices were assumed to be the single colleges listed on the mail questionnaire. For other students, initial choices were determined in the telephone interviewing phase. About 1 percent of the respondents to the follow-up survey did not enroll in any college in the fall of 1984 and an additional 1 percent enrolled in colleges other than the ones initially named in the mail and telephone surveys.

This very high degree of congruence between choices reported in the spring and fall attendance was unexpected in view of reports of admissions officers concerning "no-shows"—students who defer choices by accepting admissions offers from multiple colleges. We believe that our findings can be attributed largely to the timing and procedures of our telephone interviews, in which callbacks were made into mid-to-late June to undecided students. Although a sizable minority of students accepted to selective colleges appear to defer choices past the beginning of May, it appears that stable choices have been reached by nearly all students by late June.

The details and results of this follow-up study component are described in Chapter 9.

Concluding remarks

Our results indicate that most colleges attend to a student's academic ability in determining whether a student receives financial aid and the size of the aid package. Furthermore, monetary considerations are important to students when they choose among colleges to which they have been admitted. However, the influence of money is relatively modest compared to other factors. The primary determinant of college choice is perceived college quality, which is demonstrated to be related to a range of objectively verifiable quality measures.

Further research is needed in the area of college search behavior. In particular, a detailed investigation of the determinants of application set formation behavior would shed considerable light on the role of costs and money in leading to a college being included in or excluded from the application set. Since any college excluded from a student's application set has no chance of being chosen, colleges obviously must attend to the determinants of this crucial decision in the college selection process.

2. A comprehensive model of college choice behavior: Theory and measurement

Previous researchers have studied college choice from a number of perspectives. Varying viewpoints naturally result in attention being directed to different sets of factors and variables that might influence college choice. The range of variables studied at one time or another includes student characteristics and background, student attitudes, student perceptions of colleges, college characteristics, money (parental income level, tuition, and financial aid), student self-reported preferences, and actual college choices of students.

In this chapter, we will develop a theoretical model of college choice behavior that is meant to be comprehensive, in the sense that it encompasses and accounts for all of these various considerations and their interrelationships. This model decomposes the college choice process into a series of interrelated stages, each component of which may be examined separately using well-established statistical analysis procedures. In conceptual terms, our theoretical college choice model views students as forming intermediate summary measures to describe various college options and then evaluating the colleges by weighing these intermediate constructs. We seek to analyze which intermediate summary measures are used by students, how these mea-

sures are weighed in forming college choice decisions, and how these measures are related to and determined by actual observable characteristics of colleges (and other factors).

This multistage model is an extension of a well-established model of buyer behavior in marketing, the perception-preference-choice model (Urban and Hauser 1980; Hauser, Tybout, and Koppelman 1981; Tybout and Hauser 1981). Similar modeling efforts may be traced back to the lens model (Brunswik 1952). Information integration theory (Anderson 1974, 1981, 1982) provides a similar multistage perspective on complex judgment and evaluation processes, such as the college choice process.

Preliminary remarks

It is desirable to begin by noting several definitions that will be used in developing this comprehensive multistage model of college choice behavior.

College search and choice behavior

The college selection process is composed of two general phases: *college search* and *college choice*. For our purposes, "search" will be deemed to have ended when a student submits applications to a set of colleges. After the colleges make their admissions decisions, the "choice" phase begins. Choice is, by definition, the process by which students choose a single college to attend from among those to which they have been admitted. For choice to occur, a student must have been admitted to at least two colleges. (Students who apply to only a single institution have made important college selection decisions within the college search phase. As such, these students would be beyond the scope of the current study, since search behavior is not analyzed here.)

In studying choice, it may be implicitly assumed that all colleges being considered are at least minimally satisfactory on all major dimensions of choice; otherwise, they presumably would have been screened out during the earlier search phase. (This is not true for the cost dimension, since the complete costs associated with attending a particular college are not known to the student until after a college's financial aid decision has been made and communicated.) Thus, a compensatory or trade-off model of behavior seems viable here. In such a compensatory modeling framework, a student is implicitly viewed as weighing the various considerations associated with college choice and trading off lesser performance on some dimensions for greater performance on others.

Application set formation and choice behavior

In studying choice behavior, we assume that the application set of colleges has already been formed. We propose to study only the later stages of college selection: college choice behavior. Thus, we are unable to examine how search efforts may have influenced and shaped the ultimate college choice outcome.

This limitation in studying college choice behavior is important. It may lead to apparently anomalous results. For example, it is possible that distance (from a college's campus to a student's residence) may turn out to be an irrelevant factor at the level of college choice. This would seem to fly in the face of the empirical "fact"

that most students attend colleges near their homes. This apparent anomaly may be resolved by noting that such a distance factor, if it exists, presumably has a major bearing on the set of colleges to which a student applies. Since all colleges in a student's application set are likely to be minimally acceptable on the distance dimension, finding that distance is irrelevant at the level of choice is, indeed, possible. Such a finding results from the major screening influence that the search and application formation set decision processes exert on the college choice process.

Costs represent a second potential example of how the earlier processes of college search and application may influence choice behavior study findings. In analyzing choice behavior (as defined above), we may find that costs are of secondary importance to other factors. This finding might result because colleges that are perceived by the students (or their parents) to be too costly are screened out at the application formation stage, so that choice ultimately revolves around colleges which are minimally acceptable on the cost dimension. One counterargument regarding this cost finding is that students do not know their complete costs when they apply to colleges, since the financial aid packages are not known until the admissions and aid offers are communicated by the college to the student. Students may, of course, form expectations as to their financial aid awards and, thus, their net costs.

Individual differences

Individual differences may arise in two ways in this model of college choice behavior: different kinds of students may perceive the world differently or students may value what they perceive differently. Here, "different kinds" of students would be described by demographic, attitudinal, and other background variables.

In studying individual differences, we seek to expand upon the work of Chapman (1979), whose study of college choice behavior uncovered some important differences across different student segments, where the segments were defined in terms of students' planned academic field of study (engineering and science, liberal arts, and fine arts) and in terms of parental income levels. In this empirical effort, we wish to be sensitive to the possibility that important individual differences may exist.

In this study, we introduce another aspect of individual differences to the study of college choice behavior: context effects. For example, students choosing between high-priced private institutions only and, alternatively, among high-priced private institutions and a local public institution are expected to exhibit different choice processes. Costs for the former group are presumably less important than for the latter group. Our college choice model and empirical analyses are designed to be sensitive to assessing the presence of such choice-context individual difference effects.

An overview of a multistage model

The organization of our multistage model of college choice behavior is depicted in Figure 2.1. The three main components of this model describe the interrelationships between perception judgment formation, preference judgment formation, and choice behavior.

Students are presumed to form perceptions of colleges based on the actual physical (objectively verifiable) attributes/characteristics of the colleges and on the information they possess about a college. Here, "information" includes both the source of the information and its content. Since any finite set of college attributes may not easily be able to capture all aspects of perception, the presence of college-specific ("brand name") influences on perceptions are postulated. Finally, individual differences may exist, in that certain stu-

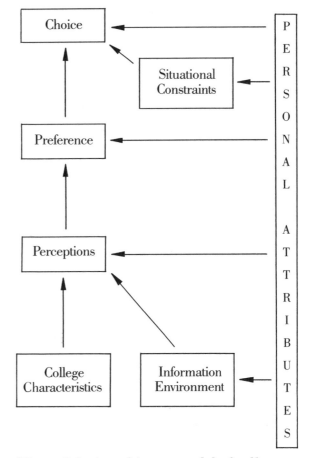

Figure 2.1. A multistage model of college-choice behavior

dent groups may perceive colleges differently or weigh their perceptions differentially.

The process by which students evaluate colleges is split into two parts in our multi-stage model: preference formation and choice behavior. This is done for several reasons. We wish to reserve the treatment of financial considerations for the choice phase. Also, we wish to ignore, for the moment, the constrained nature of choice, in that a student may choose only from among those colleges who admitted him or her. Thus, in the preference phase, we wish to have students report on their preferences for college alternatives under the assumptions that money was irrelevant and that they were admitted to all colleges to which they applied. One final differentiating feature between the unconstrained preference and choice phases may be noted: unconstrained preferences are self-reported by the students, while choice refers to actual student behavior.

The splitting of the college evaluation process into two parts is done primarily to isolate the financial aid and cost considerations (classified as being among the situational constraints in this model) in the college choice process. By including most factors other than money in the preference stage, it is expected that it will be easier to identify the role that financial considerations play in college choice behavior.

Analysis at the choice phase is based on revealed preference behavior. Actual college choice is observed, and we wish to infer the relative importances of unconstrained preferences and situational constraints—such as financial considerations (costs and financial aid)—on choice behavior. As always, individual differences may exist here. Income levels (relative to college costs) are perhaps the most important individual difference possibility to be explored.

We now turn to discussing the perception, preference, and choice phases in more detail. Data requirements, measurement issues, operationalization, and estimation approaches are explored fully in the following sections of this chapter.

Perception judgment formation

In the perception judgment formation stage, we seek to model the process by which college perceptions are formed. We postulate that a student's perception of a college depends on the actual physical (objectively verifiable) character-

istics of a college (e.g., size); objectively verifiable interactions between the student and the college (e.g., the distance from the student's residence to the college's campus); college-specific effects not otherwise captured by a college's physical attributes (e.g., "brand name" effects); and the information the student possesses about the college, including the source and content of that information. It is presumed that this linkage between how the world actually is (the objectively verifiable attributes of the colleges) and how it is perceived (the self-reported perceptual-rating scales) exists, although we are likely to have considerably less than perfect success in such a statistical modeling exercise due to the inevitable fallibility of our rating-scale measures and our inability to include all possible determinants of perceptions in any statistical model.

In mathematical terms, this may be expressed as follows:

$$R_{scd} = R(X_c, Y_{sc}, CSE_c, I_{scd}) \qquad (1)$$

where

$\quad s \quad$ a student

$\quad c \quad$ a college

$\quad d \quad$ a perceptual dimension

$\quad R_{scd} \quad$ the perceptual rating (score) student s gives to college c along perceptual dimension d (for $d = 1,2,\cdots,D$)

$\quad X_c \quad$ the physical (objectively verifiable) attributes for college c

$\quad Y_{sc} \quad$ the physical (objectively verifiable) interactions between student s and college c

$\quad CSE_c \quad$ a college-specific effect for college c: the distinctive brand-image of college c which is not adequately captured by the perceptual-rating variables

$\quad I_{scd} \quad$ the information student s possesses (and the corresponding information sources consulted by student s) about college c on dimension d.

College attributes, or characteristics, include both academic and nonacademic features. Academic dimensions of interest would include the quality of the academic enterprise plus the breadth of course/major/program offerings. Under the nonacademic category, a range of lifestyle considerations would merit attention. Extracurricular activities, diversity of student body, and campus location are but three of the potential nonacademic features to which students may direct their attention when choosing among colleges.

Parental educational background and distance (from a campus to a student's residence) are potential individual–institution interactions of note. If a parent attended a college, this extra information source might influence a student's perception of a college (positively or negatively). Distance may influence perceptions negatively, since it may act as a surrogate for uncertainty as to where a college really stands on a perceptual dimension. Of course, the college search phase presumably is focused on sorting out these kinds of uncertainties.

College-specific effects may exist in the perception formation stage. Any finite set of college attribute measures may not fully capture all the distinctiveness of a specific college. It may be necessary to include college-specific indicator variables to measure the incremental influence of the college, above and beyond that which is captured by the other independent variables.

Information possessed and information sources consulted by students about specific colleges are particularly difficult aspects of perception formation to measure in the context of a study of college choice. Since the college choice process begins at the point at which the application set is formed, there is a delicate problem concerning direction of causality. Are perceptual scores really a function of information—as our model postulates—or are self-reports on information content formulated to reflect perceptual scores? It would appear that the disentangling of these effects would require measures of the information component of the perception process at a stage or stages earlier than when the application set is formed.

In estimating the model in equation (1), it is important to note that the simple regression of the independent variables on a raw ratings-scale measure makes a very strong assumption—namely, that the students' choice sets all consist of more or less the same college alternatives. Furthermore, such a regression-modeling approach presumes that the students use approximately the same standards for rating colleges. That is, they are assumed to use the same ratings scale for deciding on when a college is "excellent" versus when it is only "good." More sophisticated model forms may be required to capture the relativeness inherent in the reporting of perceptions. The essence of perceptual ratings is relativeness, not absoluteness. Since perceptual ratings scales are only relative themselves, choice of a model form for the perception formation stage must take this consideration into account.

To combat this potential ratings-scale heterogeneity problem, our analysis approach will include standardizing the ratings of the college for each student prior to estimation of the perception judgment formation model. Such within-respondent standardizations are recommended in analyses such as this one (cf. Dillon, Frederick, and Tangpanichdee 1985).

Preference judgment formation

Preference, as used here, denotes the overall evaluation of the worth of a college alternative from the point of view of a student. Preference is postulated to depend on perceptions. In addition, constrained preferences are presumed to depend on individual-institution interactions and college-specific influences. Unconstrained preference considers all factors *except* financial ones, which are reserved for treatment at the choice phase due to their inclusion among the situational constraints facing a student.

The general form of the preference judgment formation process is as follows:

$$UPP_{sc} = UPP(R_{sc1}, \cdots, R_{scd}, \cdots, R_{scD}; Y_{sc}; CSE_c) \quad (2)$$

where

s a student

c a college

UPP_{sc} the unconstrained prior preference probability of student s for college c

R_{scd} the perceptual rating of college c by student s on dimension d (for $d = 1,2,\cdots,D$)

Y_{sc} the individual–institution variables which relate student s and college c

CSE_c a college-specific effect for college c: the distinctive brand-image of college c which is not adequately captured by the perceptual ratings variables (an indicator variable for college c, which equals 1 for college c and zero otherwise).

The perceptual views of the student are presumably the major determinants of preference. Students are viewed as forming preferences (values) about colleges based on how they perceive the colleges. That is, judgments about the world are viewed as depending on how the world is seen (perceived). For reasons of parsimony, it may be appropriate to combine raw perceptual variables into composite indices at the statistical-modeling stage.

Among the relevant individual–institution interactions at the preference judgment formation stage, special familiarity effects and distance may play significant roles. Special familiarity effects include whether either parent of a student attended a college. It is presumed that such legacy effects result in a net positive influence on students' inclinations toward such colleges. Distance (from a student's residence to a college campus) may influence students either positively or negatively. Greater distance represents more separation from family and friends and also has cost components associated with it. These factors suggest that more distance may be judged negatively. On the other hand, distance may be positively perceived since, holding everything else constant, high school seniors may wish to see new places and experience new parts of the country. These desires may be fulfilled by traveling some distance from home to attend college.

The college-specific effects are included in the preference judgment formation model to account for the inevitable measurement errors in the perceptual ratings. These variables will account for notable individual college effects that are not fully captured in any finite set of fallible perceptual ratings.

Since preference is a relative construct, a statistical model that explicitly takes relativeness into account is required. The multinomial logit model will be adopted here. This model is described in detail in Appendix 1.

Choice behavior

The variables of interest at the choice behavior stage include unconstrained preference probabilities, financial considerations, other situational constraints, and post-admissions contacts.

The general form of the choice model is as follows:

$$PC_{sc} = PC(UPP_{sc}, M_{sc}, CSE_c, PAC_{sc}, SC_{sc}) \quad (3)$$

where

s a student

c a college

PC_{sc} the probability that student s will choose to attend college c

UPP_{sc} the unconstrained prior preference probability of student s for college c

M_{sc} the money variables—costs (tuition, room and board, and other expenses), financial aid (scholarships, loans, and part-time jobs), and parental income—relating individual s and college c

CSE_c a college-specific effect for college c: the distinctive brand-image of college c which is not adequately captured by the unconstrained prior preference probability (an indicator variable for college c, equals for college c and zero otherwise).

PAC_{sc} post-admissions contacts (by letter, by telephone, and in person) of college c with student s

SC_{sc} situational constraints which affect student s when considering the choice of college c.

UPP (unconstrained prior preference probability) plays a crucial role in this choice behavior component of the multistage college choice model. It is meant to summarize all the variables, and their associated effects, described in the preference judgment formation phase. By including UPP in the choice behavior component, all the variables in the preference judgment formation phase do not have to be included here. This leads to a substantially simpler model form with considerably fewer variables, less co-linearity across variables, and correspondingly easier interpretation of the resulting relative-importance weights. UPP is, of course, expected to have a major influence on choice behavior.

UPP, the unconstrained prior preference probability, would be estimated using the model in equation (2). An alternative operationalization for UPP might involve using several indicator variables representing whether an alternative was a first, second, or third choice, for example, at the prior preference stage.

One obvious situational constraint is the composition of the choice set itself. Students may choose only to attend colleges to which they have been admitted. Financial considerations represent another kind of situational constraint. Monetary considerations include gross costs of attending a college (tuition, room and board, and other expenses) and financial aid offered by a college (scholarships, loans, and part-time jobs). The influence of income level may be an important individual-difference aspect.

Once again, college-specific effects, proxied by college-specific indicator variables, may be present in the choice stage. These "brand name" effects may not have been fully captured by the unconstrained prior preference probability measures.

Post-admissions contacts initiated by a college may have an influence on students' behavior, and the effects of such contacts will not, by definition, have been captured in the unconstrained prior preference judgments. Estimation of the influence of post-admissions contacts depends crucially on knowing who initiated a contact: the student or the college. A direction-of-causality problem arises if the student was the initiator. In such a case, it is impossible to determine with a single post-choice question of contact incidence whether the student's interest resulted in the initiation of the contact or the contact changed the student's interest level in a college. Campus visits are perhaps the most visible of the post-admissions contact activities. (See Chapter 8 for some results related to the incidence and influence of campus visits and post-admissions contacts.)

Since choice involves choosing among a finite set of alternatives, relativeness of choice is paramount. Our goal is to estimate the relative importance of unconstrained prior preference probability, money, college-specific effects, and post-admissions contacts on final college choice behavior. We will adopt the multinomial logit model form to estimate the relative importances of these factors, as revealed by students' actual choice behavior. This widely used brand choice model permits quantitative estimates of the relative importance parameters to be derived. In addition, the model form permits detailed policy analysis and assessment to answer questions related to how choice probabilities are influenced by changes in financial aid. This multinomial logit model is described in Appendix 1.

Other approaches to studying college choice behavior[1]

Single-stage versions of this multistage college-choice model have been developed by previous researchers (see, for example, Kohn, Manski, and Mundel (1976); Chapman (1977, 1979); Punj and Staelin (1978); and Manski and Wise (1983). The most famous study in the college choice domain is undoubtedly the Manski and Wise (1983) effort using data from the National Longitudinal Study of 1972. The scope of their study and the advanced statistical modeling tools brought to bear in studying college-going and college choice behavior are particularly notable.

Manski and Wise's choice model was a single-stage one of the form

choice = f (college attributes, money,
　　　　　　 other factors).

Thus, the possibility of perceptual distortions could not be detected. The size of their data base permitted the exploration of the presence of individual differences in a limited way, with reference to demographic variables only. Also, Manski and Wise had only limited financial aid information (for the college to which the student matriculated). They had to statistically impute financial aid offers of competing colleges.

While our study seeks to investigate some of the same questions of interest, it represents a number of important advances over Manski and Wise. First, the quality of our data is excellent, particularly with regard to financial aid informa-

tion. Second, our data reflect recent college choice behavior and the financial aid awarding behavior of colleges. Third, our college choice modeling framework is considerably richer than that of Manski and Wise. Our model is a much more general version of their single-stage choice model. While a multistage model has substantially greater data collection and estimation costs associated with it, the potential benefits—in terms of greater understanding of the forces which operate during the college choice process—are substantial.

Methodological considerations in estimating relative-importance weights

The three components of the college choice model—perception formation, preference judgment formation, and choice behavior—involve estimating relative-importance weights: what considerations are important and how important they are. These relative importances describe how a number of variables are related to perceptions, preferences, and choices. Two kinds of approaches exist for establishing such relative importances: self-reported weighting procedures and statistically derived weighting procedures.

Self-reported weighting procedures

Self-reported weighting procedures involve asking survey respondents to report ("self-estimate") how important various factors are to them in some decision-making, evaluation, or judgment context. Sometimes respondents are asked to identify the most important considerations from a lengthy list of possibilities. These multifactor rating tasks have a long history in marketing and survey research. For example, a number of perceptual dimensions might be described and the respondents might be asked to rate the relative importance of each in the context of choosing a college.

---

1. The remaining sections of this chapter deal primarily with a variety of methodological issues associated with college choice and enrollment research. These sections are not essential to an understanding of the research findings presented later in this report.

A major advantage of such self-reported weights is that they are individual-specific. Such self-reported weights are gathered at the level of an individual respondent, thus explicitly acknowledging the possibility of individual differences (respondent heterogeneity). A second major advantage associated with such weighting procedures is ease of measurement and analysis. The researcher has only to develop a list of potential factors that might be relevant in a choice situation, by using exploratory research techniques and by scanning the existing published literature, and then display the list to respondents. Simple arithmetic means of the scales or percentages of most frequently chosen factors suffice to summarize the results.

Some serious problems exist, however, in using self-reported weights in complex decision-making and evaluation processes, like college choice. Re-spondents may not know their own relative-importance weights, or they may not be able to easily articulate their weights during a survey. Respondents may report that everything is important, thus defeating the purpose of estimating such weights: to determine the trade-offs that decision makers are prepared to make. Finally, such self-reported weights do not lend themselves to policy analysis questions, such as how changes in financial aid might influence choice probabilities (actual enrollment behavior).

Some self-reported relative-importance results from a large ongoing survey of students (Astin et al. 1983, 1984, 1985) are reported in Table 2.1. As may be noted, college-quality considerations ("has a good academic reputation," "graduates get good jobs," and "graduates go to top grad schools") dominate the results, holding down the top three positions. Financial considerations are

Table 2.1. The determinants of college choice behavior: An example of self-reported importance considerations from the published literature

Reason	Percentage reporting the reason as very important in choosing the college that was selected		
	1983	1984	1985
Has a good academic reputation	49	52	55
Graduates get good jobs	44	44	46
Graduates go to top grad schools	24	25	26
Has low tuition	20	20	21
Has a good social reputation	20	21	23
Offered financial assistance	19	18	20
Offers special education program	18	18	22
Wanted to live near home	17	16	18
Advice of guidance counselor	8	8	8
Friend suggested attending	6	7	7
Athletic department recruited me	6	6	5
Relatives wanted me to attend	6	6	6
Teacher advised me	4	4	4
Not offered aid by first choice	n/a	4	4
College rep recruited me	3	3	4

Source: Astin et al. (1983, 1984, 1985).

the fourth and sixth highest-rated considerations ("has low tuition" and "offered financial assistance"). These ratings appear to have remained quite stable from 1983 through 1985.

In attempting to make use of such self-reported relative-importance weights, the admissions and financial aid planner has received only some directional information. It is not possible to use such ratings data to determine, for example, *how much* financial aid might offset a less desirable academic quality evaluation. More precise and sophisticated statistical modeling and analysis is required to address such questions.

Statistical weighting procedures

Statistically derived weighting procedures involve estimating the relative-importance weights using statistical procedures. Rather than using self-reported weights, the weights are statistically determined to be maximally consistent with some observed (behavioral) phenomena. Thus, for example, we observe students actually choosing certain colleges from sets of specific colleges to which they are admitted. Based on these observed choices, we then attempt to work backward and to infer how some variables describing the choice alternatives (e.g., college quality or financial considerations) were implicitly weighed by the students in arriving at their actual observed final choices.

In the college choice domain, the multinomial logit model has been used extensively to analyze the forces which influence college choice behavior (see Kohn, Manski, and Mundel 1976; Chapman 1977, 1979; Punj and Staelin 1978; and Manski and Wise 1983 for examples). By using formal statistical models in connection with a statistically derived weighting procedure, it is possible to provide a mechanism for assessing the quantitative trade-offs that students implicitly make between, say, college quality and financial considerations.

Statistically derived weighting procedures are typically based on pooling a number of survey respondents' data, thereby implicitly assuming homogeneity of the relative importances across the pooled survey respondents. It is necessary to be sensitive to the possibility of, and to statistically test for, respondent heterogeneity. Simple pooling tests exist for performing such assessments (e.g., see Chapman and Staelin 1982 and also the discussion in Appendix 1).

The multinomial logit model is used in this study to estimate the relative-importance weights for college choice behavior and prior preference formation. See Appendix 1 for an overview of some key aspects and features of the multinomial logit model.

Data collection for a multistage model

This multistage model of college choice behavior has much more extensive data requirements than the typical matriculant and admitted applicant surveys with which college admissions officials are familiar. Some remarks comparing the multistage model and typical matriculant and admitted applicant surveys seem appropriate.

The most inexpensive form of research on college choice behavior would be a matriculant survey. In such a survey, a college might survey its matriculants once they have arrived there. Matriculant surveys are quick and inexpensive to conduct, especially if they are administered in a mass fashion, perhaps during an on-campus orientation period at the commencement of classes. However, the data derived from such surveys are of extremely questionable quality. The surveys are conducted too long after the actual college choice decisions were made, so memory lapses and faulty recall are likely to be serious impediments to "clean" data collection. Also, cognitive dissonance (self-rationalization) considerations suggested that self-reported weights and college perceptions may be severely contaminated. Finally, there is a serious sampling problem in matriculant surveys: only the students who chose a college are included. The students who rejected the college are not included in the population for comparison purposes.

An admitted applicant survey corrects the sampling bias problem inherent in matriculant surveys. In admitted applicant surveys, all of a college's admitted applicants are contacted, thus resulting in the inclusion of both matriculants and nonmatriculants in the study population. The single contact point for such admitted applicant surveys is typically between late April and early June, after the choice decision has been made but well before students actually enroll at the chosen colleges. Some problems, however, continue to exist with admitted applicant surveys. First, such studies are typically done by individual colleges, and the findings usually are not publicized due to competitive considerations. Second, since colleges survey only their own admitted applicant pool, even if the study results were made public, issues related to generalizability would arise. Third, a single postchoice retrospective survey may encounter considerable problems with memory lapses, faulty recall, and postchoice rationalizations (of the form "I'm going to the college, so I must like it"). Fourth, issues of direction-of-causality arise between perceptual ratings and preference/choice: is preference/choice a function of perceptual ratings, or is it the other way around? Such issues cannot be resolved with a single-stage surveying effort which asks respondents to provide both ratings of colleges' performance/standing on a number of dimensions and overall rankings of the colleges rated.

Our multistage model of college choice behavior requires that data be collected at more than one point during the choice process. In particular, data on perceptual ratings and preferences must be collected before a student learns of admissions and financial aid decisions, and before actual college choices occur. A second wave of data collection is necessary after the final college choice is made, in the style of an admitted applicant survey. However, this second wave focuses only on measuring the actual college choice, the composition of the choice set (the colleges to which the student was ultimately admitted), and the financial aid awards made to the student by all colleges to which he or she was admitted. In addition, to satisfy the requirements of generalizability, the study population must be all high school students, not just the applicants (admitted or otherwise) to a particular college or group of colleges. With the support of the College Board, we were able to use SAT takers as the population. These considerations guided the data collection effort, which is described in Chapter 3.

College choice modeling and admissions yield rates

To further indicate how our statistical model of college choice behavior relates to typical admissions and financial aid research efforts of individual colleges, we may note that yield rates are of considerable interest to those who manage aspects of the admissions and financial aid processes. Such yield rates typically are calculated in selected pairwise competitive situations and involve examining the actual outcomes in overlap admissions situations. For example, if 100 students were admitted to both colleges A and B, and 40 of these students ultimately chose to attend college A, then college A's yield rate is 40% in competition with college B. (Note that college B's yield rate might be 35 percent, the remaining yield accruing to other colleges that were not included in the pairwise overlap admission between colleges A and B.) An admitted applicant survey provides the necessary data to estimate

Table 2.2. Some national norms for enrollment success rates (yield-rate percentages)

	National	New England	Middle States	South	Midwest	Southwest	West
		Regional breakdown					
Four-year public colleges							
Fall 1982	57.9	47.1	45.2	63.5	59.5	67.8	64.7
Fall 1983	56.3	53.8	43.3	60.5	58.3	69.4	58.8
Four-year private colleges							
Fall 1982	48.0	41.7	46.3	51.0	50.8	64.4	48.7
Fall 1983	47.9	42.1	45.3	50.3	51.6	66.8	48.6

Source: College Entrance Examination Board, *Annual Survey of Colleges 1984–85: Summary Statistics* (1984).

such yield rates. Necessary data include application set composition information, admissions decision outcomes for each college in a student's application set, and the student's final college choice.

Aggregate yield rate is the percentage of all admitted students who attend a college. Some norms for aggregate yield-rate data across various college segments are displayed in Table 2.2.

Our statistical modeling efforts are designed to attempt to explain the determinants of such yield rates. We seek to determine, in particular, how financial aid and other factors (such as college quality) influence college choices—which, when aggregated across a group of students, become yield rates. A yield rate is, after all, only an aggregate statistical summary measure. Admissions and financial aid planners require information on how they might be able to influence yield rates if they are to cope with the many demands associated with thoughtful, efficient, and effective admissions and financial aid decision making and planning.

3. Study design and data collection

The design of the study and the associated data collection effort followed from the formulation of the comprehensive multistage college choice model described in the previous chapter. We begin this chapter by describing the design of the two-stage surveying procedure, the data requirements, and sources of data for our college choice modeling effort. Sampling procedures used in the study will then be discussed. A nonrespondent bias analysis is conducted and reported. The chapter concludes with a brief statistical overview of the student population which comprises this study.

Study design, data requirements, and data sources

The two-stage surveying procedure adopted in this study included an initial mail survey and a follow-up telephone survey. The mail survey was conducted in March 1984, after the students had formed their application sets but before most actual college choices had been made. The follow-up telephone interviews occurred in May/June 1984, after the college choice process had concluded. Appendixes 2 and 3, respectively, contain the wording of the questions on the mail and telephone interview surveys.

The data requirements to estimate the various components of this comprehensive multistage college choice model are described in Table 3.1.

Sampling procedure

For our purposes, we were interested in high-ability high school seniors, since these would be the students most likely to attract no-need financial aid. In this study, high-ability students were drawn from the 1983–84 high school graduating class. Students were included in our population if they (1) scored 550 or more on the SAT (average of verbal and mathematical scores); (2) were in the top fifth of their high school class (self-reported on the Student Descriptive Questionnaire associated with the SAT); and (3) were U.S. residents.

Based on survey response rates in past college choice research efforts, and the requirements for the statistical analysis in this study, an overall sample size of 2,000 was selected.

A disproportionate stratified random-sampling procedure was used in this study. Students with average (mathematical and verbal) SAT scores in the ranges 550–599, 600–649, 650–699, 700–749, and 750–800 were sampled with equal frequency. Thus, a total of 400 students were included in each of these 50-point ranges on the SAT. The effects of this disproportionate sampling plan on depth-of-population strata sampled is described in Table 3.2. As may be noted, while we sampled

Table 3.1. Data requirements and sources

Data requirement	Source
Individual student differences:	
—Demographic characteristics, high school experiences, and college plans	College Board records: SAT registration and the SDQ
—Financial status variables	College Board records: CSS Report
—Student SAT scores	College Board records
Student perceptions of colleges	Mail survey (and telephone survey, for comparison purposes)
Student self-reported importance weights	Mail questionnaire (and telephone survey, for comparison purposes)
College characteristics	College Board records: *The College Handbook* data base (1985 edition)
College price data	College Board records: *The College Handbook* data base (1985 edition)
Unconstrained preferences	Mail survey
Financial aid awards	Telephone survey
Post-admission contacts	Telephone survey
Actual college choices	Telephone survey

only 0.9 percent of the students in the 550–599 range, our design included 51.1 percent of the students in the top SAT group, the 750–800 range. This concentration of sample points in the top SAT ranges was deliberate, since these students were most likely to receive large no-need aid awards. Thus, we wished to oversample these students, relative to their natural incidence in the

Table 3.2. Sample sizes in various SAT strata

SAT score interval	Strata size	Sample size	% of strata population sampled
550–599	46,504	400	0.9
600–649	32,545	400	1.2
650–699	16,439	400	2.4
700–749	5,331	400	7.5
750–800	781	400	51.2

population, in order to have ample presence of such financial aid at the analysis stage.

The results of our surveying procedure are described in Table 3.3. The 77.5 percent response rate to the mail survey is excellent, even given the generally high norms (in the 40–60 percent range) for admitted applicant surveys. Of the 1,549 respondents to the mail survey, 325 (21.0 percent) applied to only one college (typically under an early action, early decision, rolling admission, or similar program). Thus, the eligible population for the second-stage telephone survey was 1,224. Ultimately, 96.7 percent of these students responded to the follow-up survey. This level of response rate to the telephone follow-up is outstanding, presumably reflecting the attention-getting value of telephone interviewing, the timing of the calls (just after the college choice decision had been made), and the general interest of the students in this study (since they had previously provided information via the mail survey).

Nonrespondent bias analysis

Although the response rates to our surveys were extraordinarily high—77.5 percent for the mail survey and 96.7 percent for the follow-up telephone survey—it is still appropriate to conduct a nonrespondent bias analysis. Our concern here is whether the respondents have different characteristics than the nonrespondents. Since we have relevant demographic variables for all 2,000 members of our population, the respondents' and nonrespondents' characteristics may be readily assessed and compared.

Table 3.4 contains a comparison of the mail survey respondents and nonrespondents along five relevant demographic variables: average SAT score, gender, planned higher educational level, planned field of study, and self-reported parental gross income. As may be noted, there are no substantial deviations between the respondent and nonrespondent groups along any of these demographic variables. Thus, these respondents appear to be representative of the original 2,000 students in the population, and a nonresponse bias problem does not appear to be present in these survey data (at least, based on this comparison of key demographic variables of the respondents and the nonrespondents).

Given the 96.7 percent response rate to the telephone survey, no formal nonrespondent bias analysis is necessary. Even if the nonrespondents were systematically different from the respondents, their small number would not materially influence our results.

Table 3.3. Results of sampling efforts: response rate analysis

Original sample size	2,000
Stage-1 respondents (mail)	1,549[1]
Students applying to only one college	325
Eligible population for Stage 2	1,224
Stage-2 respondents (telephone)	1,183[2]

1. 77.5% response rate.   2. 96.7% response rate.

A statistical overview of these students

The data reported in Table 3.4 document the background of the students in our population. A summary of the key descriptors would include the following observations.

The majority of these students are male (63.1 percent). In terms of academic field of interest, science (42.2 percent) and engineering (22.5 percent) predominate. These high-ability high school seniors have high educational aspirations, with 76.0 percent reporting graduate-level education plans. Many of the students come from relatively affluent backgrounds (38.2 percent of the students are from households where the family income is $50,000 or more).

Several other aspects of the backgrounds and accomplishments of these 2,000 high-ability high school seniors merit mention. These students primarily attend public high schools (81.3 percent). They come from family settings where education appears to be valued and a way of life: 72.4 percent (57.4 percent) of their fathers (mothers) have college degrees, while 45.8 percent (21.8 percent) of their fathers (mothers) have graduate degrees. With regard to high school athletic participation, 79.7 percent of the students competed in sports, with 35.4 percent winning one or more varsity letters. These students were also active in community groups, with 64.4 percent claiming active membership in such organizations and 24.2 percent indicating that they were major office holders.

In summary, these high-ability high school seniors are of such ability not only in a narrow academic sense. They appear to be leaders in athletic and community groups as well. They also come from high-status households, at least as measured by parental educational levels and, to some extent, by household income.

Table 3.4. Nonresponse bias analysis: Comparisons of demographic characteristics of respondents and nonrespondents to the mail survey

Demographic characteristic	Total sample	Respondents	Nonrespondents
Average SAT scores			
550–599	20.0%	19.0%	23.5%
600–649	20.0	19.5	21.7
650–699	20.0	19.5	21.7
700–749	20.0	20.9	16.9
750–800	20.0	21.1	16.2
	100.0%	100.0%	100.0%
Gender			
Male	63.1%	62.2%	66.3%
Female	36.9	37.8	33.7
	100.0%	100.0%	100.0%
Planned educational level			
Graduate school	76.0%	76.1%	75.9%
Bachelor's/uncertain	24.0	23.9	24.1
	100.0%	100.0%	100.0%
Planned field of study			
Sciences	42.2%	41.8%	43.6%
Engineering	22.5	23.0	20.8
Other	35.4	35.2	35.7
	100.0%	100.0%	100.0%
Self-reported parental gross income			
$30,000 or less	25.9%	25.1%	28.9%
$30,001–$49,999	35.9	37.0	32.0
$50,000 or more	38.2	37.9	39.0
	100.0%	100.0%	100.0%

Note: Due to rounding, some totals do not add up to 100.0%.

4. Determinants of college choice behavior

In this chapter, we report and analyze the results of our efforts to assess the determinants of college choice behavior. Choice behavior concerns how students ultimately choose one of the colleges to which they have been admitted. In our multistage perception preference choice model, the choice component begins with a prior preference for a college—a measure of college preference unconstrained by monetary considerations and other situational constraints (such as whether a student was admitted to a college). This prior preference is then attenuated by monetary considerations and other situational constraints.

Findings related to the choice component of our multistage college choice model are presented in this chapter; findings related to preference and perception judgment formation behavior in Chapters 6 and 7. We begin by presenting some descriptive statistics concerning the application set formation process. Of particular interest is the result that 21 percent of the students applied only to a single college. Next, we examine the tendency of students to actually attend their first-preference college and related matters which bear on the college choice decision. Then, we develop and estimate a statistical model (a multinomial logit model) of college choice behavior. This model seeks to determine the implicit weights (relative impor-

tances) that students place on their prior preferences and other relevant variables when they make their college choice decisions. We then investigate whether important individual differences exist, that is, whether some students weigh the prior preference and other relevant variables differentially when choosing a college. A second type of individual differences is also investigated: context effects. Context effects refer to different choice situations, such as choosing from among a choice set which contains one or more Ivy League colleges. A number of scenarios are constructed to illustrate the influence of several variables on the college choices of our students.

Some preliminary results and descriptive statistics

We begin the analysis of college choice behavior by examining some relevant descriptive statistics related to application set sizes, switching behavior, and related matters. These analyses are designed just to be exploratory in nature, to provide the backdrop for the statistical modeling efforts to follow.

The distributions of the application and choice set sizes for our survey respondents are displayed in Table 4.1. Students applied to an average of 3.6 colleges. However, about one-fifth of all these students (21.0 percent) applied to only a single college, while another one-fifth (20.2 percent) applied to six or more colleges. These 1,549 stu-

Table 4.1. Application and choice set sizes[1]

Size of set	Application set	Choice set
1	21.0%	6.3%
2	17.3	29.5
3	16.3	27.0
4	13.1	15.6
5	12.0	10.8
6	8.5	5.7
7	4.6	2.5
8	3.7	1.6
9	1.5	0.4
10+	1.9	0.6
Total	100.0%[2]	100.0%
Mean	3.6	3.4

1. The data base for the application set sizes is the 1,549 students who responded to the mail survey. The data base for the choice set sizes is the 1,183 students who responded to the telephone survey. Note that only students with application sets of greater than one were included in the second wave (the telephone survey) of this study.
2. Due to rounding, the application set total does not add to 100.0%.

dents submitted 5,298 admissions applications, and 63.8 percent of these admissions applications were accompanied by a request for financial aid.

Students who applied to more than one college received an average of 3.4 admissions offers. A considerable number of these high-ability high school seniors had relatively large choice sets: 37.3 percent of the students who applied to more than one college had choice set sizes of four or more.

As noted in Chapter 3, 21 percent of these students applied to only a single college. In the sense of college choice as used in this study, these students did not have a choice, since choice is defined as selection from a set of two or more colleges offering admission to a student. This group represents a relatively large number of students, and some further investigation of its composition seems appropriate.

Table 4.2 contains some descriptive statistics on a range of demographic variables for the single- and multiple-college applicant groups. The main differences seem to lie in average SAT scores, planned educational level, and parental income. Students in the multiple-applicant group have higher average SAT scores, are more likely to plan for a graduate level of education, and come from higher-income families. A sizable proportion of the single-college applicants are applying to public institutions, where admission is highly likely or guaranteed or where admission decisions are made on a rolling basis. It is likely that a smaller number of these students were accepted to selective colleges under some form of early action.

The choice component of our multistage college choice model begins with a prior preference measure and then adds in other relevant variables, some of which moderate this measure and some of which represent information which becomes completely known to students only after they receive their admissions offers. Our ultimate measure of choice was obtained during the telephone follow-up interview, which was conducted after the students had made their actual college choice decision.

Changes between prior preferences and final college choices must exist if post-admissions variables such as financial aid exhibit any influence on the ultimate college choice decision. For our students whose choice sets contained two or more colleges, 60.5 percent did ultimately choose to attend the college they identified as their first choice. However, the 39.5 percent of students who switched represent a large enough group to lead us to investigate the factors which led some students to change their prior preferences while others held fast to their original college prefer-

Table 4.2. Comparison of single- and multiple-college applicants

	Single-college applicants	Multiple-college applicants
Average SAT scores		
550–599	24.6%	17.5%
600–649	20.6	19.2
650–699	20.6	19.2
700–749	20.0	21.2
750–800	14.2	23.0
	100.0%	100.0%
Gender		
Male	57.8%	63.4%
Female	42.2	36.6
	100.0%	100.0%
Planned educational level		
Graduate school	64.8%	79.0%
Bachelor's/uncertain	35.2	21.0
	100.0%	100.0%
Planned field of study		
Sciences	40.2%	42.2%
Engineering	20.9	23.6
Liberal arts	20.9	18.7
Other	18.1	15.4
	100.0%	100.0%
Self-reported parental gross income		
$30,000 or less	30.3%	23.7%
$30,001–$49,999	38.3	36.6
$50,000 or more	31.4	39.7
	100.0%	100.0%

Note: Due to rounding, some totals do not add to 100.0%.

ences. Table 4.3 displays the incidence of prior preference changes for students with various sized choice sets.

The self-reported reasons for switching seem to relate substantially to monetary considerations, as the data in Table 4.4 demonstrate. About 50 percent of these switchers cited cost or finan-cial aid as a prime reason for switching. These observations must be tempered with the point that only those who switched were asked about their reasons. Conceivably, those who did not switch might have had exactly the same reasons for staying with their original choice.

One further exploratory inquiry involved asking

Table 4.3. Incidence of switching from original first-choice college

Choice set size	No. of students choosing their first-choice college	No. of students choosing another college	Incidence of switching
2	229	111	32.6%
3	185	126	40.5
4	120	59	33.0
5	51	74	59.2
6	39	28	41.8
7+	31	30	49.2
Overall	655	428	39.5%

students directly how much additional scholarship aid would be required to lead them to switch to their second-choice college (see Table 4.5 for the relevant results). We asked the students four separate questions, related to whether $500, $1,000, $2,000, or $3,000 would lead them to change their college choice. Even with the largest amount—$3,000—only about half the students reported that they would switch. These results suggest that it may take rather large financial inducements to cause students to change from their

Table 4.4. Stated reasons for not choosing the original first-choice college[1]

Reason	Frequency
Better financial aid	27.4%
Lower costs	23.1
Campus visits	12.6
Location	10.5
Academic reputation	11.9
Other	14.4
	100.0%[2]

1. The data reported in this table refer to 271 students in the telephone survey who reported their chosen college as different from their first-choice college (to which they were admitted) in the mail survey and who gave a reason for changing.
2. Due to rounding, the total does not add up to 100.0%.

otherwise first college choices. Of course, students' answers to such direct and hypothetical questioning may not necessarily be valid indicators of actual behavior, so we need another approach to assess the influence of monetary considerations on college choice. Such an approach, involving the construction and estimation of a statistical model of college-choice behavior, is described in the following section.

A multinomial logit model

We now turn to documenting our multinomial logit model of college choice behavior. In turn, we describe the formulation of the model, estimation issues, model specification analyses, and the results of explorations into individual differences analyses.

Model formulation

The variables in our choice model are described in Table 4.6. These variables form the *base model*. We will subsequently test to see if a small set of additional variables should be added to form an *extended model*.

As may be noted, there are four distinct groups of variables, corresponding to unconstrained prior preference measures, financial constraints and considerations, individual–institution inter-

Table 4.5. Stated choice intentions if second-choice college offered an extra scholarship

Amount of extra scholarship	Percentage whose college choice would change
$ 500	3.8
$1,000	13.2
$2,000	31.2
$3,000	49.0

actions, and college-specific effects. The theory underlying the inclusion of these groups of variables was described in Chapter 2.

To measure prior preference, three indicator variables are included in the model: FIRST, SECOND, and THIRD. These variables indicate whether a college alternative was first, second, or third in a student's original preference evaluation prior to receiving complete admissions and financial aid information from all colleges. (If a student was not ultimately admitted to his or her first-choice prior preference college, then FIRST was appropriately modified to correspond to the highest-ranked college to which the student was ultimately admitted. Similar adjustments were made for SECOND and THIRD, when necessary.) We expect that FIRST, SECOND, and THIRD will all have very strong effects on choice, since they summarize all preference-related components in our model. Naturally, FIRST should have the greatest influence on choice, followed consecutively by SECOND and THIRD. With regard to the financial variables, incomplete data (total financial aid without the grant and non-grant components; missing data on perceived renewability of aid; occasional missing college cost data) necessitated the inclusion of several composite variables to model out missing data effects. Grant (GRANTAID) and non-grant (OTHERAID) aid are included as separate variables to account for the expected differential impact of these aid types.

Perceived renewability of aid (RENEWAL) is an interesting heretofore uninvestigated influence on college choice. We expect that COSTS will have a negative influence on choice, while GRANTAID and RENEWAL will influence a college's attractiveness in a positive fashion, other factors held constant. The influence of OTHERAID is uncertain, but presumably it is not negative. Since such aid includes loans and part-time jobs, it does not come "free"—it either has to be paid back or work must be performed to earn it. Thus, OTHERAID is presumably of much less value to the student than GRANTAID.

By including SATFIT, we may investigate the influence of "academic quality zoning" on students' choices. Note that SATFIT is really defined in terms of the lack-of-fit between the college and the student, as measured in terms of the absolute value of the difference between respective SAT scores. It is expected that higher values of SATFIT will have a negative influence on choice: students should prefer to be at colleges where the average student ability level is fairly similar to their own (as measured by SAT scores), holding other factors constant.

Seven college-specific indicator variables are included in the choice model. The top seven colleges—in terms of frequency of mention in the original applications of our 1,549 mail survey respondents—are denoted COLLEGE1, COLLEGE2, . . . , and COLLEGE7. Each of these colleges had at least 150 mentions across the 1,549 application sets. The specific identities of the colleges are not crucial to our investigation; suffice it to say that they are well-known, highly visible, selective private institutions located largely, but not exclusively, in the northeast of the United States. Recall that the inclusion of these college-specific variables is designed to model out "brand name" effects that might not otherwise be fully captured by other variables in the model (chiefly the prior preference variables). Such alternative-specific indicator variables are typically

Table 4.6. *Definition of the variables included in the choice model*

Variable	Definition

Unconstrained prior preference

FIRST — An indicator variable denoting whether a college was the first-choice in the original preference ranking (in March): equals 1 if this college was the first-choice prior preference college, and equals 0 otherwise.

SECOND — An indicator variable denoting whether a college was the second-choice in the original preference ranking (in March): equals 1 if this college was the second-choice prior preference college, and equals 0 otherwise.

THIRD — An indicator variable denoting whether a college was the third-choice in the original preference ranking (in March): equals 1 if this college was the third-course prior preference college, and equals 0 otherwise.

Financial constraints and considerations

COSTS — Total costs (in $000s) to attend a college; includes tuition, room and board charges, and other expenses. If costs are missing, then COSTS = 0.

COSTSM — An indicator variable for missing total costs: equals 1 if COSTS are missing (COSTS = 0), and equals 0 otherwise.

TOTALAID — Total financial aid (in $000s), if only a total aid figure was reported and individual aid breakdowns into grant and non-grant aid were not available; equals 0 otherwise.

GRANTAID — Grant aid (in $000s) if separate grant and non-grant breakdowns were reported; equals 0 otherwise.

OTHERAID — Other aid (in $000s)—non-grant aid (loans and part-time work)—if separate grant and non-grant breakdowns were reported; equals 0 otherwise.

RENEWAL — Self-reported perceived renewal possibility for financial aid; coded as 1 = "None," 2 = "Possible," 3 = "Probable," and 4 = "Certain" if renewal possibility was reported, and equals 0 otherwise. (If no aid was awarded, then RENEWAL is set equal to 0.)

RENEWM — An indicator variable for missing values of RENEWAL; equals 1 if RENEWAL is missing, unknown, or unreported (RENEWAL = 0), and equals 0 otherwise. If a student receives no aid, then RENEWM is set equal to 1.

Individual–institution interactions

SATFIT — The SAT "fit" between a college and a student; equals the absolute value of the difference between the student's SAT score and the average SAT score of all students at a college if both SATs are available, and equals 0 otherwise.

SATM — An indicator variable which equals 1 if a college's mean SAT scores were not available, and equals 0 otherwise.

College-specific effects

COLLEGE1 — An indicator variable that equals 1 for the most frequently mentioned college in terms of applications submitted by our 1,549 mail survey respondents, and equals 0 otherwise.

COLLEGE2 through COLLEGE7 — Indicator variables for the second through seventh most frequently mentioned colleges in terms of applications submitted by our 1,549 mail survey respondents.

included in choice models such as the one being constructed here (c.f. Ben-Akiva and Lerman 1985).

Descriptive statistics for each of the variables in Table 4.6 are displayed in Table 4.7. These statistics are for the 3,882 college alternatives in the 1,101 choice sets that were available for analysis. Seven of the 1,108 students with choice-set sizes of at least two included tied first-choice colleges. These were not used in the analysis.

The following are observations about the summary statistics reported in Table 4.7:

- Some of the 1,101 choice sets had ties reported for the second-choice college. This accounts for the mean value of SECOND exceeding that of FIRST.
- The mean total costs of attendance at the colleges to which these 1,101 students were admitted was $10,494, ignoring the 35 college alternatives out of a total of 3,882 (0.9 percent) for which college cost data were missing. Thus, these students are obviously opting in substantial numbers to apply to the selective, well-known, expensive private colleges.
- With regard to perceived renewability, 64.2 percent of the 3,882 college alternatives to which our 1,101 students were admitted had missing data. Only 3.1 percent of these were aid awards where the students did not report a value for perceived renewability; the other 61.1 percent correspond to non–aid award situations, where perceived renewability is irrelevant (and where, by definition, RENEWAL = 0).
- The average difference between college and student SAT scores, averaged over all the choice alternatives to which the students were admitted, was 91.7.
- By summing the mean values for COLLEGE1, . . . , COLLEGE7, it may be noted that only about 16.4 percent of these college alternatives were the seven most frequently mentioned colleges. That is, about one-sixth of the 3,882 admissions

Table 4.7. Descriptive statistics for variables in the choice model

	Summary statistics	
	Mean	Standard deviation
FIRST	0.213	0.410
SECOND	0.223	0.416
THIRD	0.181	0.385
COSTS	10.494	4.248
COSTSM	0.009	0.095
TOTALAID	0.065	0.666
GRANTAID	1.239	2.344
OTHERAID	0.503	1.197
RENEWAL	1.003	1.408
RENEWM	0.642	0.479
SATFIT	91.706	62.999
SATM	0.072	0.259
COLLEGE1	0.025	0.156
COLLEGE2	0.024	0.154
COLLEGE3	0.023	0.151
COLLEGE4	0.025	0.156
COLLEGE5	0.024	0.152
COLLEGE6	0.016	0.125
COLLEGE7	0.027	0.161

Note: These descriptive statistics are based on all choice set alternatives for the 1,101 choice sets which were used to develop the multinomial logit model of college choice behavior.

offers to these 1,101 students were from the top seven colleges.

Preliminary analysis

A useful preliminary analysis of our choice data is reported in Table 4.8. Means for selected variables from Table 4.6 are shown for first-choice colleges (the colleges actually chosen), second-choice colleges, third-choice colleges, and other colleges. Some interesting and apparently predictable patterns seem to emerge.

	Overall[2]	First-choice (chosen) college alternatives	Second-choice college alternatives	Third-choice college alternatives	Other college alternatives
COSTS	10.494	10.794	10.551	10.378	10.164
GRANTAID	1.239	1.863	1.056	0.969	0.936
OTHERAID	0.503	0.745	0.451	0.422	0.341
RENEWAL	1.003	1.310	0.959	0.822	0.837
SATFIT	91.706	77.394	87.352	95.417	110.880
COLLEGE1	0.025	0.052	0.022	0.013	0.006
COLLEGE2	0.024	0.035	0.021	0.024	0.016
COLLEGE3	0.023	0.043	0.025	0.011	0.008
COLLEGE4	0.025	0.051	0.023	0.008	0.011
COLLEGE5	0.024	0.031	0.028	0.023	0.011
COLLEGE6	0.016	0.015	0.022	0.013	0.012
COLLEGE7	0.027	0.027	0.033	0.031	0.016

1. In this table, "choice position" refers to the actual final ranking of alternative colleges to which students were admitted. Thus, "first-choice (chosen)" refers to the college actually chosen by the student; "second-choice" refers to the college the student reported he or she would attend if not attending the first-choice college.
2. Means listed under the "Overall" column are taken directly from Table 4.7. They are reported here for comparative purposes and to assist in the interpretation of the other means reported in this table.

COSTS decrease slightly as we move from first-choice to other high-choice colleges. For example, the average first-choice college has total costs of $10,794, while the average third-choice college has total costs of $10,378. This small decrease is noteworthy: It appears that the high-cost private and the low-cost public college options are sprinkled throughout these students' choice sets, rather than concentrated at the top or bottom. This would also suggest that costs are not too crucial a factor at the level of college choice.

Note that COSTS and other variables in Table 4.8 are being examined one at a time, rather than simultaneously. Viewed in this fashion, higher costs appear to be slightly positively associated with choice, presumably because many colleges perceived by students to be desirable on other grounds are also costly. We expect that when the effect of costs is estimated simultaneously with other variables that costs will turn out to be negatively associated with choice.

The mean GRANTAID and OTHERAID decrease as we move from first-choice to other high-choice colleges. For example, the mean GRANTAID offered by first-choice colleges was $1,863, while that offered by third-choice colleges was only $969—a reduction of about $900. Since COSTS only decrease by a small amount (about $400 between first- and third-choice colleges), college costs do not account for the differences in average grant amounts from first- to third-choice colleges. These data suggest that GRANTAID (and, perhaps to a lesser extent, OTHERAID) has an influence on choice behavior.

RENEWAL drops sharply as we move from first-choice (mean RENEWAL value of 1.310) to third-choice (0.822) college alternatives. This is consistent with students paying considerable attention to perceived renewability of financial aid awards when they make their college-choice decisions. This evidence is consistent with the view that as perceived renewability decreases, so does the choice probability associated with a particular college alternative.

SATFIT increases considerably from first-choice (mean SATFIT value of 77.394) to third-choice (95.417) college alternatives. This is consistent with students preferring to attend colleges where the average SAT score of the other students is similar to their own.

As noted earlier, about 16.4 percent of the 3,882 college alternatives confronting our 1,101 students were from the top seven colleges (in terms of frequency of mention). This concentration increases to 25.4 percent when we look only at first-choice college alternatives. Not surprisingly, the colleges attracting the largest number of applications are also chosen by students with high frequency.

In summary, this preliminary analysis suggests that GRANTAID, RENEWAL, and the college-specific indicator variables have positive influences on choice probabilities. Lack of SAT fit (as measured by the variable SATFIT) appears to have a negative influence on choice probabilities.

Model estimation

A multinomial logit model was estimated using the variables described in Table 4.6. A linear additive functional relationship was assumed. The results of this estimation are displayed in Table 4.9.

The results reported in Table 4.9 are for an explosion depth of one. That is, only the first-choice rank-ordered choice sets were used in the estimation. Attempts to use the second- and third-ranked colleges to form additional choice sets, as described in Chapman and Staelin 1982,

were unsuccessful. In testing whether the second-choice ranking could be used, the conclusion was that explosion to a depth of two was not appropriate. (Thus, higher-order explosions were not investigated.) The relevant chi-squared test statistic value was 84.8 (with the corresponding critical chi-squared value of 36.2, for 19 degrees of freedom and a 1 percent level of significance). Thus, we reject the null hypothesis that the first and second explosion depths yield equivalent relative-importance weights. Apparently these students use a different weighting system from that used for the actual college chosen for evaluating second- and possibly subsequent-choice alternatives in their rank ordering.

The log-likelihood ratio index (LLRI) value of 0.419 is exceptionally high for such college-choice studies. As noted in Appendix 1, values of LLRI in the 0.10–0.35 range are typical in college choice studies employing the multinomial logit model. This LLRI value appears to exceed those achieved in other published studies of college choice behavior (where noncollege alternatives are not considered.) This high level of statistical performance presumably follows from our efforts to carefully collect the relevant data at the key points in the college choice process. The relatively homogeneous nature of our sample—consisting of high-ability students—may also have contributed to this result, since these students may have been more consistent in their choice behavior than would a more heterogeneous sample.

Several other measures of the goodness-of-fit (statistical performance) of our model were developed. We may use the statistical model to predict our students' actual college choices and then compare such predictions to actual college enrollment levels for our sample. In such an analysis, the unit of investigation becomes the college, rather than the student.

The correlation between predicted and actual college enrollments, when aggregated across all

Table 4.9. Results of estimating the choice model

Variable	Coefficient estimate	Standard error	T-Ratio
FIRST	3.2762	0.1693	19.346
SECOND	1.9061	0.1589	11.992
THIRD	1.3063	0.1616	8.085
COSTS	−0.1313	0.0195	−6.716
COSTSM	−0.0400	0.5105	−0.078
TOTALAID	0.0770	0.1113	0.692
GRANTAID	0.2907	0.0360	8.068
OTHERAID	0.0158	0.0550	0.029
RENEWAL	0.3062	0.1344	2.279
RENEWM	0.6075	0.3909	1.554
SATFIT	−0.0041	0.0015	−2.754
SATM	0.0631	0.2548	0.248
COLLEGE1	2.0964	0.3314	6.326
COLLEGE2	1.2433	0.3323	3.742
COLLEGE3	1.7104	0.3351	5.105
COLLEGE4	1.5709	0.3222	4.875
COLLEGE5	0.6886	0.3336	2.064
COLLEGE6	0.8403	0.4214	1.994
COLLEGE7	−0.0676	0.3123	−0.216

Summary statistics
Number of choice sets = 1,101
Initial log-likelihood = −1289.6
Final log-likelihood = −749.0
Log-likelihood ratio index = 0.419

Note: Refer to the discussion in Appendix 1 for details and interpretations of the various log-likelihood statistics.

1,101 students, was 0.856. The average percentage absolute error in prediction across the 24 colleges with at least ten actual enrollments from our sample of students was 11.1 percent. ("Percentage absolute error" for a single college equals 100.0 times "absolute error" divided by the actual enrollment value. Absolute error equals the absolute value of the predicted enrollment minus the actual enrollment.) For the 60 colleges with at least five actual enrollments, the corresponding average percentage absolute error was 16.2 percent. Thus, in aggregate, we are able to predict college choices of these high-ability students with a high degree of precision.

Model-specification analysis

In addition to the variables described in Table 4.6, some other variables were of interest as potential determinants of college choice behavior. Because our prior feelings about these variables were less strong than those about the variables in Table 4.6, we have reserved these variables for specific statistical testing to determine if they should be added to the base model. Our general philosophy is to seek a parsimonious (simple) model form, unless strong evidence exists to support the embracing of a more complicated model form (with, for example, more variables).

The additional variables are described in Table 4.10. FATHER and MOTHER measure the potential of legacy effects to influence choice. DISTANCE proxies the costs (monetary and psychological) associated with travel to a distant college. APPNOAID represents the possible negative effect of a college denying financial aid to an aid applicant. PFIRST, PSECOND, and PTHIRD are interactive variables between portable (personal) scholarship aid—such as National Merit Scholarships that are awarded to the student for use at whatever college he or she chooses—and prior preference. Inclusion of these variables in the model was designed to check on a hypothesis that students with relatively large amounts of portable aid would be more likely than others to act consistently with their prior preferences, since monetary considerations would be less constraining. Of course, such students might have applied to

different colleges in the first instance. Finally, to assess the possibility of financial aid exerting a nonlinear influence on college choice (rather than the linear effect postulated by the base model), quadratic terms for the two key aid variables—GRANTAID and OTHERAID—were aided to the model.

The results of the statistical tests for the several groups of variables are reported in Table 4.11. In all cases, the extra variables did not add significantly, given that the base-model variables (described in Table 4.6) were already included in the multinomial logit model of college choice behavior. Thus, we conclude that none of these variables should be added to the base model.

It is interesting to note that parental legacy effects, portable scholarship aid, distance, and the effect of applying for but being denied aid at a college apparently are not relevant factors at the level of college choice. The parental legacy and distance effects may, of course, have been influential at the search stage in leading to the colleges to which students applied in the first instance. However, at the choice stage, they appear to have no residual influence.

Table 4.10. Other variables tested in the extended choice model

Variable	Definition
FATHER	An indicator variable that equals 1 if a student's father attended a college, and equals 0 otherwise.
MOTHER	An indicator variable that equals 1 if a student's mother attended a college, and equals 0 otherwise.
DISTANCE	The distance (in 000s of miles) from the campus of a college to the residence of a student.
APPNOAID	An indicator variable that equals 1 if a student applied for and was denied aid at a college, and equals 0 otherwise.
PFIRST	Amount of portable (personal) scholarship aid (in $000s) times FIRST.
PSECOND	Amount of portable (personal) scholarship aid (in $000s) times SECOND.
PTHIRD	Amount of portable (personal) scholarship aid (in $000s) times THIRD.
GRANT2	Equals GRANTAID*GRANTAID.
OTHER2	Equals OTHERAID*OTHERAID.

Group of variables tested	Calculated test statistic	Degrees of freedom	Critical value	Conclusion[2]
FATHER, MOTHER	2.6	2	9.2	n/s
DISTANCE	3.2	1	6.6	n/s
APPNOAID	0.2	1	6.6	n/s
PFIRST, PSECOND, PTHIRD	5.4	3	11.3	n/s
GRANT2, OTHER2	0.4	2	9.2	n/s

1. A 1 percent level of statistical significance was used in these tests.
2. Under "Conclusion," "n/s" means that the calculated test-statistic value does not exceed the critical value, so the null hypothesis (that the indicated group of variables has no influence on college choice) cannot be rejected. Thus, such variables should not be added to the model, since the most parsimonious representation corresponds to the model without such variables.

Interpretation of the choice model results

Based on the choice model results reported in Table 4.9, the main determinant of college choice appears to be prior preference. Financial considerations are relevant, but they are clearly secondary. Also, perceived renewability of aid awards and SATFIT are statistically significant in the predicted directions. The college-specific effects appear to be quite substantial, as well. In summary, these students appear to take many things into account when choosing colleges.

A number of quantitative comparisons may be made using the coefficient estimates to illustrate and interpret the results. Given that the focus of this study is on no-need scholarship aid, it will be useful to interpret these results in terms of implicit equivalent amounts of scholarship aid.

Since our multinomial logit model is essentially a utility or value model, it will be convenient to interpret a coefficient estimate times the value of the corresponding variable as representing (partial) utility points. For example, based on the results reported in Table 4.9, a typical student derives 3.2762 utility points from a first-choice prior-preference college. Such a student derives

(0.2907) (5.000) = 1.4535 utility points from a $5,000 scholarship aid offer. A college with costs of $10,000 would be interpreted as yielding (−0.1313) (10.000) = −1.313 utility points for a typical student. Here, the negative sign on the COSTS coefficient signifies that higher-cost colleges are, holding other things constant, less preferred (i.e., students receive less utility or value from higher-cost colleges, *ceteris paribus*).

The difference between a first- and second-choice prior preference college is 1.3701 utility points (3.2762 − 1.9061). Since each $1,000 of scholarship aid is implicitly evaluated as being equivalent to 0.2907 utility points, a second-choice college that offers an extra $4,713 scholarship would just offset the difference between being the second choice and being the first choice on a prior preference basis. For a third-choice prior preference college that wishes to compete with a first-choice college, an extra scholarship of 1,000*(3.2762 − 1.3063)/0.2907 = $6,776 would be required to bring it up to par with the first-choice college. This illustrates that money will "buy" students, but it seems that the cost associated with this is quite substantial.

With regard to the financial variables, each $1,000 of total costs penalizes a college 0.1313 utility points, while each $1,000 of scholarship aid adds 0.2907 utility points to the overall utility or value of a college. This suggests that about $2 of extra costs may be approximately offset by $1 of scholarship aid. However, we are operating at the choice stage here: Too expensive colleges—from the perspective of the student or the student's parents—might have been ruled out of consideration at an earlier stage, prior to submitting applications to colleges.

Non-grant aid (OTHERAID) appears to have no detectable influence on choice behavior. It neither adds to nor subtracts from the overall desirability of a college.

Perceived renewability is weighed positively by students when they evaluate colleges. Each extra point of perceived renewability yields an additional 0.3062 utility points for a school. Also, the relative values of the coefficients on RENEWAL and RENEWM suggest that these students implicitly evaluate no information about renewability as being approximately equal to a value of 2 (0.6075/0.3062) on our four-point renewability scale (where "2" = "Possible"). A $5,000 scholarship with no chance of being renewed yields a total utility of (5.000)(0.2907) + (1)(0.3062) = 1.7597, taking only the scholarship and renewability into account. An $1,840 scholarship with guaranteed renewability would yield approximately the same amount of utility. Thus, it seems that students implicitly discount nonrenewable scholarship aid to a substantial extent. These results suggest that colleges should extend a considerable amount of effort in specifying renewability conditions in the clearest possible terms. If a student is in doubt, he or she may implicitly downgrade a college's financial aid offer, especially compared to aid offers which the student perceives to have high chances or to be guaranteed of being renewed.

With regard to SATFIT, each 100 points of SAT difference (between the student's SAT score and the average SAT score of all students at a college) reduces the value of a college by 0.41 utility points. This is approximately equivalent to the value of a scholarship of $1,410.

The college-specific effects are substantial, ranging from about 0 to 2.1 utility points. The average college-specific effect (for the top seven colleges in terms of frequency of mention) is equal to 1.155 points. This is approximately equal to the value of a scholarship of $3,972. Thus, in a choice set with just two colleges, a non-"top seven" college would have to offer a scholarship of $3,972 to be approximately equivalent in utility terms to an average top seven college (assuming that all other things were equal).

The missing data correction factors—COSTSM, TOTALAID, and RENEWM—are, in general, not statistically significant. Thus, they have no impact on the model's results; however, they do serve to account for these missing data effects.

These and other related examples will be described later in this chapter, when we investigate more fully the implications of these findings about the determinants of college choice.

Individual differences analyses

The relative-importance weights results reported in Table 4.9 are for all students. To assess whether students' backgrounds influence their choice weights, and to assess whether these weights are stable across different choice situations, individual differences analyses may be conducted. These analyses require the use of statistical-pooling tests—for example, are the relative-importance weights of men identical (in a statistical sense) to those of women? The framework of these pooling tests for the multinomial logit model is described in Appendix 1.

Demographic variables. We tested for heterogeneity of weights for the following demographic variables (and subgroups of students): SAT scores ("average SAT score less than or equal to 675"; "average SAT score more than 675"), gender ("male"; "female"), planned educational level

Table 4.12. Individual differences analysis: Pooling test results for demographic variables[1]

	Calculated test statistic	Degrees of freedom	Critical value	Conclusion
Average SAT scores (2 groups)	24.2	19	36.2	n/s[2]
Gender (2 groups)	19.6	19	36.2	n/s
Planned educational level (2 groups)	10.8	19	36.2	n/s
Planned major field of study (3 groups)	44.8	38	61.1	n/s
Parental income (3 groups)	65.8	38	61.1	Significant

1. A 1 percent level of statistical significance was used in these tests.
2. Under "Conclusion," "n/s" means that the calculated test-statistic value does not exceed the critical value, so the null hypothesis that the groups have identical relative-importance weights cannot be rejected; "significant" means that the groups apparently are characterized by different relative-importance weights.

("bachelor's or uncertain"; "graduate school"), planned major field of study ("sciences"; "engineering"; "other"), and parental income level ("$30,000 or less"; "$30,001–$49,999"; "$50,000 or more"). The results of these tests are displayed in Table 4.12.

The pooling test results shown in Table 4.12 indicate that only in the case of parental income level are the relative-importance weights different. Thus, we may conclude that the weights reported in Table 4.9 adequately describe all SAT levels (in the range represented in our sample, 550–800), men and women, all planned major fields of study, and all planned educational levels (bachelor's only versus graduate school intentions). There are no apparent individual differences based on these demographic variables. However, since significant differences exist across parental income groups, a detailed examination of these differences in appropriate.

Parental income effects. The coefficients for the various parental income groups are shown in

Table 4.13. Also, for reference purposes, means of selected choice model variables for the groups are displayed in Table 4.14. Major differences across the parental income groups are described below.

The impact of GRANTAID is great on low-income students (0.4448 utility points per $1,000 of scholarship), less for medium-income students (0.2236 per $1,000), and then great again for high-income students (0.4064 per $1,000). OTHERAID appears to be irrelevant for all groups. The low- and medium-income coefficients on GRANTAID follow a predictable pattern: As income increases, there is less sensitivity to financial considerations. However, the influence of GRANTAID is almost as great for the high-income as it is for the low-income group.

The rise in the GRANTAID effect as we move from the medium- to the high-income group may, in the first instance, appear odd. The data in Table 4.14 indicate that the average GRANTAID of $548 for high-income students is considerably

Table 4.13. *Coefficient estimates for different parental income levels*

	All students with reported parental income	Income groups		
Variable		Low income (less than $30,000)	Medium income ($30,001 to $49,999)	High income ($50,000 or more)
FIRST	3.4108**	3.2068**	3.4437**	3.7543**
SECOND	2.0608**	1.7946**	2.1517**	2.1749**
THIRD	1.4487**	1.5682**	1.4897**	1.3350**
COSTS	−0.1439**	−0.1962**	−0.1815**	−0.1260**
COSTSM	−0.1803	−1.9300	1.0438	1.2213
TOTALAID	0.1032	0.2276	0.2027	−1.0860
GRANTAID	0.2964**	0.4448**	0.2236**	0.4064**
OTHERAID	−0.0131	0.0525	0.0222	−0.1494
RENEWAL	0.4340**	0.7650*	0.4506**	0.1597
RENEWM	1.0189*	2.3328*	0.5931	0.6266
SATFIT	−0.0044**	0.0002	−0.0024	−0.0118**
SATM	−0.0206	0.5215	−0.0247	−0.5516
COLLEGE1	1.9919**	2.6034**	1.8458**	1.9592**
COLLEGE2	1.3756**	1.6991	1.4773*	1.2436*
COLLEGE3	1.7753**	0.8033	2.0738**	1.8866**
COLLEGE4	1.6666**	3.1201**	1.6991**	1.3267*
COLLEGE5	0.6535	0.4572	1.0031	−0.0451
COLLEGE6	1.0268*	0.6286	2.5554**	0.1730
COLLEGE7	0.0171	0.0978	−0.1141	0.1120
Summary Statistics				
No. of choice sets	976	228	359	389
Initial LL	−1138.2	−255.4	−420.0	−462.8
Final LL	−652.1	−145.1	−245.7	−228.4
LLRI	0.427	0.432	0.415	0.506

Note: Refer to the discussion in Appendix 1 for details and interpretations of the various log-likelihood statistics. Significance at the 1 percent [5 percent] level is denoted by "**" ["*"] (one-tailed test).

smaller than the corresponding figure for low-income students ($2,228). Thus, the high-income students must be responding to the psychological impact of receiving scholarships: it's not just the money, it's the recognition that goes along with receiving such scholarship aid. Further support for this recognition-effect interpretation may be found by looking at the relationships among other coefficients across income groups. High-income students are much less sensitive to COSTS than are low-income students, so monetary considerations are not that important in and of themselves. Also, high-income students do not particularly value renewability of aid, at least not to the extent that low-income students do.

There are important differences in terms of the

Table 4.14. *Means of selected choice model variables, by income groups*

Variable	All students with reported parental income	Income groups		
		Low income (less than $30,000)	Medium income ($30,001 to $49,999)	High income ($50,000 or more)
COSTS	10.449	9.842	10.062	11.140
GRANTAID	1.275	2.228	1.493	0.548
OTHERAID	0.512	0.900	0.635	0.184
RENEWAL	1.008	1.495	1.219	0.544
SATFIT	90.965	85.238	95.085	90.371
COLLEGE1	0.025	0.017	0.021	0.032
COLLEGE2	0.025	0.014	0.018	0.036
COLLEGE3	0.023	0.014	0.018	0.032
COLLEGE4	0.025	0.018	0.018	0.034
COLLEGE5	0.021	0.013	0.022	0.025
COLLEGE6	0.015	0.009	0.011	0.022
COLLEGE7	0.026	0.023	0.029	0.025

impact of COSTS as we move across the income groups. Each $1,000 of cost represents a reduction of 0.1962 utility points for a low-income student, while the corresponding figures for medium- and high-income students are 0.1815 and 0.1260, respectively. This drop in importance in COSTS as income increases is consistent with the expected relationship between financial status and sensitivity to financial considerations. However, note that even for the high-income students, COSTS are a significant factor in the college choice decision.

The influence of perceived renewability is greatest for low-income students (0.7650 utility points per perceived renewability-scale point), next highest for medium-income students (0.4506 utility points per perceived renewability-scale point), and apparently irrelevant for high-income students. Once again, this pattern is consistent with lower-income students having the greatest sensitivity to financial considerations.

The influence of SATFIT on choice is statisti-cally significant only for high-income students: Each point in SAT difference represents a decrease of 0.0118 utility points. Thus, a 100-point SAT difference would correspond to a decrease of 1.18 utility points. The model predicts that such a 100-point difference for a high-income student could be overcome with a scholarship of approximately $2,904.

As income increases, so does the concentration of colleges in the top seven. The data in Table 4.14 indicate that about 10.8 percent of the low-income students' college alternatives are concentrated in the top seven, while the corresponding figures for medium- and high-income students are 13.7 percent and 20.6 percent, respectively. (These percentages are the sums of the means of the indicator variables for the top seven colleges.) However, the coefficient estimates for the various income groups reported in Table 4.13 suggest that the overall importance of the top seven college-specific effects does not change systematically across the various income groups. The mean col-

Table 4.15. Choice context effect groups

	Group definition	Number of choice sets
"Ivy League" effect[1]		
Group 1: IVY-0	All choice sets containing zero Ivy League colleges.	665
Group 2: IVY-1	All choice sets containing one Ivy League college.	226
Group 3: IVY-2 +	All choice sets containing two or more Ivy League colleges.	210
		1,101
"COFHE" effect[2]		
Group 1: COFHE-0	All choice sets containing zero COFHE colleges.	488
Group 2: COFHE-1	All choice sets containing one COFHE college.	256
Group 3: COFHE-2 +	All choice sets containing two or more COFHE colleges.	357
		1,101

1. The "Ivy League" schools were defined to include the traditional Ivy League institutions (Brown, Columbia, Cornell, Dartmouth, Harvard, University of Pennsylvania, Princeton, and Yale), plus MIT and Stanford.
2. The "COFHE" colleges and universities consist of the 30 institutions that are members of the Consortium on Financing Higher Education. The members of COFHE include Amherst, Barnard, Brown, Bryn Mawr, Carleton, Chicago, Columbia, Cornell, Dartmouth, Duke, Harvard and Radcliffe Colleges, Johns Hopkins, MIT, Mount Holyoke, Northwestern, University of Pennsylvania, Pomona, Princeton, Rochester, Smith, Stanford, Swarthmore, Trinity, Vanderbilt, Washington University, Wellesley, Wesleyan University, Williams, and Yale.

lege-specific effect for the top seven colleges is 1.3442 for low-income students, with the corresponding figures for medium- and high-income students being 1.5058 and 0.9509, respectively.

Thus, in summary, there appear to be predictable patterns of change in relative-importance weights as income increases: sensitivity to financial considerations generally decreases as income increases.

Context effects. In assessing the possibility of individual differences based on choice-context effects, we are interested in exploring variation in relative-importance weights for students who face different types of choices. The question of interest is: Do students who face certain kinds of choices and choice sets weigh things differently than other students?

To test for context effects, we split our 1,101 choice sets into a number of non-overlapping subgroups. The specific context effects that we chose

to investigate are displayed in Table 4.15. The "Ivy League" and "COFHE" effects address the possibility that students who are considering well-known, nationally prominent, private (expensive), and selective college alternatives may differ from students who do not face such choices. Furthermore, as the concentration of these kinds of schools in a choice set changes, so might the relative-importance weights on the determining factors.

The Ivy League schools are, of course, well known. The COFHE schools were chosen as a separate category to denote a larger group of nationally prominent private colleges and universities. See the notes to Table 4.15 for precise definitions of which institutions were included in these groups.

The relevant pooling test results are reported in Table 4.16. In each case, the null hypothesis is that the coefficients are equal for each of the

Table 4.16. Results of the context-effects individual-differences analysis[1]

Context effect analyzed	Calculated test statistic	Degrees of freedom	Critical value	Conclusion
"Ivy League" effect	30.6	31	52.2	n/s[2]
"COFHE" effect	30.0	31	52.2	n/s

1. A 1 percent level of statistical significance was used in these tests.
2. Under "Conclusion," "n/s" means that the calculated test-statistic value does not exceed the critical value, so the null hypothesis that the groups have identical relative-importance weights cannot be rejected.

groups. The rejection of this null hypothesis would be consistent with the presence of context effects; that is, relative-importance weights do differ by choice situation.

The results reported in Table 4.16 indicate that Ivy League and COFHE context effects are not present here. Apparently, our high-ability students use about the same relative-importance weights in choosing colleges regardless of the degree of concentration (composition) of their choice sets with Ivy League and COFHE institutions.

Further context-effects testing (e.g., for students primarily choosing among small colleges) was not possible due to limitations of available data. Finer breakdowns of choice sets than the examples tested here would have yielded groups of data with insufficient numbers of choice sets to permit the estimation of a multinomial logit model in each subgroup. With a model of our size (19 variables), a minimum of several hundred choice sets are needed to permit estimation with suitable levels of statistical precision (Chapman and Staelin 1982).

Concluding remarks regarding individual differences. The general robustness of our relative-importance weights is especially notable. Of the various individual difference possibilities examined, only differences in the relative-importance weights related to income were detected. No other individual difference or context effects are apparently in evidence here.

In essence, these results suggest that high-ability students—regardless of demographic background (except for income) or choice context/setting—are consistent in their implicit views as to the relative weights of the various factors evaluated during the college choice decision-making process. Thus, our relative-importance weights in Table 4.9 appear to be widely applicable to high-ability students of the type studied here and in the range of college choice contexts typically present for such students.

Interpreting the choice model results

To provide further interpretation of the choice model results, we now turn to constructing a number of examples (cases, scenarios, illustrations) to apply these results. Our primary interest here is in examining how choice probabilities are determined in various circumstances, and especially how financial aid influences such choice probabilities.

The various choice-probability calculations which follow all use the multinomial logit model described in Chapter 2 (and Appendix 1), as it was operationalized and estimated in this chapter, as well as the coefficient estimates reported in Table 4.9 and, for individual differences, in Table 4.13. As will become apparent, these probabilities depend on the choice situation—what colleges are available and where the colleges stand in terms of the multinomial logit model's variables (described earlier, and listed in Table 4.6).

To illustrate the method of calculating the various choice probabilities under various scenarios, Appendix 4 contains a detailed numerical example. The illustrative examples used in the remainder of the chapter will, in general, be considerably less complicated than the example described in Appendix 4.

Preliminary definitions and discussion

In the various examples that follow, the term "effective cost of scholarship aid" (or some variant) is used frequently. It is important to clarify and define this term precisely, since it is of great importance in interpreting the choice model results.

As is discussed in these examples, we find that a $1,000 scholarship is estimated to move an indifferent student (one who is equally inclined toward each of two colleges) from 50–50 choice probabilities to 57.2–42.8 percent choice probabilities, in favor of the college awarding the extra $1,000 scholarship. What is the actual and effective cost of a college awarding such a student a $1,000 scholarship?

The actual cost of such a scholarship is, of course, $1,000 to a student who ultimately chooses to enroll at the college. However, this does not take in account several considerations, chiefly the likelihood of the student enrolling even in the absence of a scholarship.

To move toward a determination of the "effective cost of scholarship aid," we may begin by noting that the initial expected enrollment probability for the "indifferent" student described

above is 50.0 percent. A $1,000 scholarship increases the expected enrollment probability from 50.0 percent to 57.2 percent. For a student who actually chooses to enroll, the scholarship cost is $1,000 to the college. However, not all students actually enroll. Furthermore, some of such scholarships (actually 50 percent in this case) will inevitably go to students who ultimately would have chosen to enroll at the college even in the absence of the $1,000 scholarship.

The "effective cost of scholarship aid" may be defined as the expected cost of scholarship aid (which equals the amount of the scholarship aid multiplied by the enrollment probability in the presence of the aid) divided by the change in enrollment probability induced by the scholarship aid. Thus, in our example, the effective cost of scholarship aid is (1000) (0.572)/(0.572 − 0.500) = $7,944. Thus, effective cost per additional student is considerably above actual cost.

Another way to arrive at this result is to consider a group of 100 such students. With no aid, 50 would be expected to enroll. With $1,000 aid offered to all 100 students, the cost of such a scholarship program would be $57,200, corresponding to the $1,000 scholarships claimed by each of the 57.2 students who enroll. Thus, the extra 7.2 students "cost" $57,200 in scholarship aid, or $7,944 per extra student.

The intuition behind this effective cost of scholarship aid figure is as follows. Much of the aid is awarded to students who would have chosen to enroll at the college even in the absence of the aid. Furthermore, the use of the $1,000 of scholarship aid only marginally improves the college's chance of being chosen (from 50 percent to 57.2 percent).

Several other considerations about this definition of "effective cost of scholarship aid" should be noted. First, this is defined on a per-year basis. The implicit multi-year nature of financial aid awards at most colleges—students in good academic standing being eligible for "like" aid in subsequent years—means that the effective cost of scholarship aid should probably be multiplied by four, to reflect the overall financial commitment from the college's viewpoint. Second, the effective cost of scholarship aid does not take tuition income into account. The tuition income generated by a student enrolling at a college offering such aid would serve to partially offset the cost of the aid to the college.

Example 1: Prior preferences and choice probabilities

We begin by assessing the influence of prior preferences on choice probabilities. Suppose the following situation exists:

Choice set composition	Two colleges, denoted as colleges A and B.
Prior preference situation	College A is the first-choice prior preference college alternative; college B is the second-choice prior preference alternative.
Financial considerations	Colleges A and B are equal on COSTS, GRANTAID, and OTHERAID.
College-specific considerations	Colleges A and B are not top seven colleges (or, equivalently, it may be assumed that they are both average top seven colleges).
Other relevant factors	Colleges A and B are equal on RENEWAL and SATFIT.

In this situation, our statistical model would predict that the student would choose the highest-preference college with a probability of 79.7 percent. (Results for students in specific income groups are: low-income, 80.4 percent; medium-income, 78.4 percent; and high-income, 82.9 percent.)

If we change the choice situation slightly to include college C (the third prior preference college) and assume everything else is equal, then the estimated choice probabilities would be 71.8

percent, 18.2 percent, and 10.0 percent for the first, second, and third prior preference colleges, respectively.

These examples clearly demonstrate the very strong influence of prior preferences on choice behavior. It takes a lot to overcome the inherent advantage associated with being a student's first-choice prior preference college. This finding, of course, means that it is important to examine the determinants of prior preference; this will be done in Chapter 6.

Example 2: Prior preferences, financial aid, and choice probabilities

We now extend Example 1 and consider how scholarship aid might be used to offset the disadvantage of not being the first-choice prior preference college. We use the same basic situation as described in Example 1:

Choice set composition	Two colleges, denoted as colleges A and B.
Prior preference situation	College A is the first-choice prior preference college alternative; college B is the second-choice prior preference alternative.
Financial considerations	Colleges A and B are initially equal on COSTS, GRANTAID, and OTHERAID. However, as discussed below, college B will offer an "extra" scholarship.
College-specific considerations	Colleges A and B are not top seven colleges (or, equivalently, it may be assumed that they are both average top seven colleges).
Other relevant factors	Colleges A and B are equal on RENEWAL and SATFIT.

We now ask: How much extra scholarship aid—above and beyond that already offered—would the second-preference college have to offer to increase its chances of being chosen to 50 percent? Our results suggest that an *extra* scholarship of about $4,713 would be required. This result may be extended to our three income groups: low income, $3,175; medium income, $5,778; and, high income, $3,886. This illustrates the relative sensitivity of the low- and high-income groups to scholarship aid, compared to the medium-income group.

As noted earlier, it is apparently possible to "buy" students to overcome the disadvantage of not being the first-choice prior preference college alternative; however, it does appear to be fairly expensive to do so.

Example 3: Scholarship aid and choice probabilities

Another view of the influence of scholarship aid on choice probabilities may be gained by examining the influence of aid alone on choice, holding everything else constant. This situation is described as follows:

Choice set composition	Two colleges, denoted as colleges A and B.
Prior preference situation	Colleges A and B are equal in prior preference (i.e., tied for first-choice prior preference position).
Financial considerations	Colleges A and B are initially equal on COSTS, GRANTAID, and OTHERAID. However, as discussed below, college B will offer an "extra" scholarship.
College-specific considerations	Colleges A and B are not top seven colleges (or, equivalently, it may be assumed that they are both average top seven colleges).
Other relevant factors	Colleges A and B are equal on RENEWAL and SATFIT.

This situation corresponds to a student facing a two-alternative choice set where, considering all relevant factors, the student is indifferent between the two colleges. Thus, the probability of choosing each college is 50 percent: the student is equally likely to attend either college. Another

interpretation of "indifference" (or 50–50 choice probabilities) is that this reflects our basic uncertainty about being able to predict which college a student will ultimately choose.

Now, suppose that one of the colleges offers the student an *extra* amount of scholarship aid (above and beyond the aid already offered). Our next question is: How much would the choice probability shift if an extra scholarship award were offered? The shifts in choice probabilities for various amounts of extra scholarship aid offered are shown in Table 4.17. As its illustrative calculations indicate, large amounts of scholarship aid ($5,000) can move a 50–50 percent choice situation to an 81–19 percent situation, when all other factors are held constant. However, a $5,000 extra scholarship would presumably have to be renewed for an additional three years, thus representing a total outlay of $20,000. Furthermore, the $5,000 in extra scholarship really translates into an effective cost of $13,039 per year. Here, effective cost is calculated as follows: probability changes from 0.500 to 0.811 for $5,000 of aid, so effective cost is $(5000) (0.811)/(0.811 - 0.500) = \$13,039$ per year, or $52,156 for four years (exclusive of the offset provided by tuition fees).

The "holding other things constant" condition, the two-alternative choice set assumption, and the assumption of equal prior preferences for the two colleges are all crucial to the interpretation of these figures. Later in this chapter we will investigate more realistic situations, in which these assumptions are relaxed.

Example 4: Financial aid and perceived renewability

Renewability of financial aid is valued by our high-ability students. Some trade-offs in size of scholarship aid and degree of perceived renewability are indicated by the data reported in Table 4.18. If a college intends its financial aid to be renewable (perhaps under certain conditions of

Table 4.17. Estimated effects of additional aid on choice probabilities

| | Amount of extra scholarship | | | | | |
	$0	$1,000	$2,000	$3,000	$4,000	$5,000
Overall	50.0	57.2	64.1	70.5	76.2	81.1
Low income	50.0	60.9	70.9	79.2	85.6	90.2
Medium income	50.0	55.6	61.0	66.2	71.0	75.4
High income	50.0	60.0	69.3	77.2	83.6	88.4

Table 4.18. Effects of perceived renewability of aid

| Amount of scholarship offered with "possible" chance of renewal | Equivalent amount of scholarship that could be offered to obtain the same overall utility, with renewal perceived as: | |
	"Probable" (RENEWAL = 3)	"Certain" (RENEWAL = 4)
$4,000	$2,947	$1,893
$4,500	$3,447	$2,393
$5,000	$3,947	$2,893
$5,500	$4,447	$3,393
$6,000	$4,947	$3,893
$6,500	$5,447	$4,393
$7,000	$5,947	$4,893

academic performance), then these figures suggest that this renewability should be clearly communicated to students. Otherwise, students may implicitly downgrade or discount a financial aid offer.

Example 5: SATFIT and financial aid

Each extra point of SATFIT can be offset by a scholarship of $14. Thus, a 100-point SATFIT value would require about a $1,400 scholarship to just cover the lack of academic fit between the student and the college.

However, SATFIT is really an important factor only for high-income students. For such students, the model predicts that each extra point of SAT-FIT may be offset by a scholarship of approximately $29. Lower-tier colleges that seek to attract high-ability students must overcome the

lack of academic fit as well as other possible disadvantages.

Toward a cost–benefit analysis of no-need aid

We now consider some further, more complicated scenarios to illustrate the effects of using no-need financial aid. In realistic choice situations where no-need aid might be offered by a college, we wish to assess the economics of using such aid. Our main concern is to document the costs associated with pursuing such a pricing strategy.

The relevant costs associated with no-need financial aid include the actual amount of the scholarship aid for those who enroll at a college due to the aid, *plus* the costs associated with

Table 4.19. Illustrative effective scholarship costs (cost–benefit analysis 1)

| Amount of extra scholarship | Expected student enrollment | Initial-year costs | | Four-year scholarship cost per incremental student |
		Total extra scholarship cost	Scholarship cost per incremental student	
$ 0	50.0	$ 0	$ 0	$ 0
$1,000	57.2	$ 57,200	$ 7,944	$31,776
$2,000	64.1	$128,200	$ 9,092	$36,368
$3,000	70.5	$211,500	$10,317	$41,268
$4,000	76.2	$304,800	$11,634	$46,536
$5,000	81.1	$405,500	$13,039	$52,156

providing such aid to students who already would have attended a college without any further no-need financial aid inducement. This latter group is typically impossible to identify ahead of time, so no-need aid must be offered to a class of students—and not just those with low probabilities of attending a college in the first instance.

Cost–benefit analysis 1: A simple scenario

Suppose that a college offers no-need financial aid awards to each of 100 students who are approximately indifferent between it and another college (in the context of a two-alternative choice set). Considering all relevant factors (except these extra no-need financial aid awards), these 100 students would split about 50–50 between the two colleges.

What are the economics (in a cost–benefit sense) of offering these students various amounts of no-need scholarship aid? Key numbers are displayed in Table 4.19, for various amounts of no-need scholarships.

In interpreting the numbers in Table 4.19, it is important to note that:

▪ The extra no-need aid cannot be targeted specifically at those who are very unlikely to attend the no-need aid awarding college. All students

must be offered such aid, even those who would have attended without it. (Of course, only some of these students will actually ultimately attend the college offering the aid.)

▪ The "four-year scholarship cost per incremental student" assumes that the aid is continued for the full four undergraduate years.

▪ These calculations do not include the extra net tuition income generated by the "incremental" students responding to the no-need scholarship aid.

These results make clear that large no-need scholarships ($5,000) will:

▪ Move many indifferent students toward the college offering such aid (81.1 percent of such students will be induced to enroll, rather than only 50 percent), and

▪ Cost a substantial amount of money, when expressed over a four-year time horizon ($52,156 per extra student attracted, before accounting for the extra tuition income that these students will provide).

Cost–benefit analysis 2: A complicated (and realistic) scenario

A typical scenario involving the use of no-need aid is for a high-cost private college to offer such financial support to compete more favorably with a low-cost public institution. Of course, other considerations (such as perceived relative college quality) may operate in favor of the private college.

To investigate the economics of awarding such aid, we will *assume that the student in question is high-income* (so no-need aid is the only kind of financial aid that could be offered) and:

	College A (private)	College B (public)
COSTS	$12,000	$5,000
GRANTAID	To be determined	No aid offered
RENEWAL	Guaranteed	Not relevant
SATFIT	100	150

All other variables not mentioned above are assumed to be equal for both colleges (except when modified in the following discussion and analysis).

In this situation, the base choice probability when college A offers $0 of no-need aid is 42.8 percent (assuming that colleges A and B are equally preferred on a prior preference basis). The disadvantage that college A faces with much higher costs is only partially offset by a better SATFIT (100 versus 150). Some alternative situations involving various amounts of no-need aid

and various prior preference situations are displayed in Table 4.20.

The last case described in Table 4.20 is particularly noteworthy. The private college that uses no-need aid to compete with an otherwise preferred (on a prior preference basis) public college can increase its choice probability from 13.3 to 54.3 percent by offering $5,000 of no-need aid. However, this really represents an effective cost per incremental student of $6,622 per year, or $26,488 over a four-year period (exclusive of tuition revenues from the student). Here, effective cost per year is calculated as follows: probability changes from 0.133 to 0.543 for $5,000 of aid, so effective cost is $(5000) (0.543)/(0.543 - 0.133) = \$6,622$ per year, or $26,488 over four years.

The full set of effective costs associated with Table 4.20 are displayed in Table 4.21. The extreme costs of the second case, where college A is the first-choice prior preference college, arise because most of the students (78.4 percent) would have attended the college with no extra no-need financial aid inducement. In contrast, the last case is relatively cost-effective for college A. Since few of the students would have attended without the no-need aid, most of the aid goes to

Table 4.20. Illustrative probabilities (cost–benefit analysis 2)

	Probability of choosing college A, if college A offers the following amounts of no-need scholarship aid					
	$0	$1,000	$2,000	$3,000	$4,000	$5,000
If colleges A and B are equally preferred on a prior preference basis	42.8	53.2	63.0	71.9	79.3	85.2
If college A is the first-choice prior preference college	78.4	84.6	89.2	92.5	94.9	96.5
If college A is the second-choice prior preference college	13.3	19.0	26.0	34.5	44.2	54.3

Table 4.21. Illustrative effective costs (cost–benefit analysis 2)

	Initial-year effective cost to college A of offering the following amounts of no-need scholarship aid				
	$1,000	$2,000	$3,000	$4,000	$5,000
If colleges A and B are equally preferred on a prior preference basis	$ 5,115	$ 6,238	$ 7,412	$ 8,690	$10,047
If college A is the first-choice prior preference college	$12,645	$16,519	$19,681	$23,006	$26,657
If college A is the second-choice prior preference college	$ 3,333	$ 4,094	$ 4,882	$ 5,722	$ 6,622

students who actually switch (and little is awarded to those who would have attended without it).

Cost–benefit analysis 3: Competition among top-tier and other private institutions

For our next scenario, suppose that a lower-tier private institution wishes to compete against a top-tier private school for high-ability students, and that no-need aid is the chosen vehicle to improve the lower-tier school's competitive situation. Here, "top-tier" is defined as "top-seven" and "lower-tier" is defined to be not in the top-seven college group. What are the economics associated with such competition?

Once again, we will *assume that the student in question is high-income* (so no-need aid is the only kind of financial aid that could be offered) *and* the factors shown below:

	College A (the top-tier private college)	College B (the lower-tier private college)
COSTS	$14,000	$9,000
GRANTAID	No aid offered	To be determined
RENEWAL	Not relevant	Guaranteed
SATFIT	50	150

In addition to the above, college A is presumed to be an average top-seven institution, while college B is presumed not to be among the top-seven colleges. All other variables not mentioned above are assumed to be equal for both colleges (except when modified in the following discussion and analysis).

In this situation, the base-choice probability when college B offers $0 of no-need aid is 18.2 percent (assuming that colleges A and B were equally preferred on a prior preference basis). As may be noted, the value of college A being in the top seven and the much better SATFIT (50 versus 150) virtually overwhelm the advantage that college B has on costs.

Some alternative situations involving various amounts of no-need aid and various prior preference conditions are displayed in Table 4.22. In this situation, note that if college B is not the first-choice prior preference college, there is virtually no chance of the student choosing to attend it (4.4 percent) in the absence of no-need aid. No-need aid, of course, will increase the choice probability in favor of college B, but at considerable cost. The lower-tier private college—college B, in this example—that uses no-need aid to compete with an otherwise preferred (on a prior preference basis) top-seven private college can increase its choice probability from 4.4 percent to 26.2 percent by offering $5,000 of no-need aid. Thus, even with a $5,000 scholarship offer, our hypothetical student is still about three times as likely to choose college A as college B (73.8 percent versus 26.2 percent). The $5,000 grant represents an effective cost per incremental student of $6,009 per student per year, or $24,036 per student over a four-year period (exclusive of tuition revenues from the student). Here, effective cost per year is calculated as follows: probability changes from 0.044 to 0.262 for $5,000 of aid, so effective cost is (5000) (0.262)/(0.262 − 0.044) =

$6,009 per student per year, or $24,036 per student over four years. These results illustrate the overwhelming advantage enjoyed by a top-seven college that is also a student's first-choice college on a prior-preference basis over a lower-tier private competitor. No-need aid will improve the lower-tier college's chances of attracting high-ability students, but large amounts are required to offset the advantage enjoyed by the preferred school.

The full set of effective costs associated with Table 4.22 are displayed in Table 4.23. Once again, the effective costs associated with no-need

Table 4.22. Illustrative probabilities (cost–benefit analysis 3)

| | Probability of choosing college B, if college B offers the following amounts of no-need scholarship aid | | | | | |
	$0	$1,000	$2,000	$3,000	$4,000	$5,000
If colleges A and B are equally preferred on a prior preference basis	18.2	25.3	33.7	43.3	53.4	63.3
If college B is the first-choice prior preference college	52.0	62.2	71.2	78.7	84.8	89.3
If college B is the second-choice prior preference college	4.4	6.5	9.5	13.6	19.1	26.2

Table 4.23. Illustrative effective costs (cost–benefit analysis 3)

| | Initial-year effective cost to college B of offering the following amounts of no-need scholarship aid | | | | |
	$1,000	$2,000	$3,000	$4,000	$5,000
If colleges A and B are equally preferred on a prior preference basis	$3,563	$4,348	$5,175	$ 6,068	$ 7,018
If college B is the first-choice prior preference college	$6,098	$7,417	$8,843	$10,341	$11,971
If college B is the second-choice prior preference college	$3,095	$3,725	$4,435	$ 5,197	$ 6,009

aid awards are largest when the initial situation is already favorable to a college. The effective cost of no-need aid is minimized when it can be targeted to students who are unlikely to attend the aid awarding college without the presence of substantial no-need aid awards.

Cost–benefit analysis 4: The top-seven prior preference phenomenon

As a final illustration of the economics of no-need aid, consider the case of a high-income student with an average SAT of 650. Assume a three-college choice set, as follows:

College A: First-choice prior preference college, costs = $15,000, no aid offered, an average top-seven college, and average SAT score is 650 (so SATFIT = 0)

College B: Second-choice prior preference college, costs = $5,000, no aid offered, not a top-seven college, and average SAT score is 500 (so SATFIT = 150)

College C: Third-choice prior preference college, costs = $10,000, aid to be determined, not a top seven college, and average SAT score is 500 (so SATFIT = 150)

This scenario describes the high-ability high-income student whose first-choice prior preference college is a top-seven college and whose second and third prior preference choices (colleges B and C) are a local public college and a lower-tier private college, respectively. In this scenario, colleges B and C might be viewed by the student as "safety colleges": they were originally considered just in case the student failed to gain admission to the top-seven college.

In this scenario, colleges B and C are at a tremendous disadvantage in not being "top seven," in not being the first-choice prior preference college, and in having a poor fit in terms of SAT scores. College A is just right on SATFIT, and its only disadvantage is its high cost. This scenario seems to be a choice situation faced by

many students and one which is of interest in illustrating the importance of first-choice prior preference, of being a top-seven college, and of SATFIT, even for a college with costs of $15,000.

If college C gives $0 of no-need aid, then the choice probabilities are: college A, 94.4 percent; college B, 4.5 percent; and college C, 1.0 percent. Thus, with $0 no-need aid, college C stands virtually no chance of attracting this student. On the other hand, if college C discounts its cost to this student by 50 percent by a guaranteed renewable $5,000 grant, the choice probabilities change to: college A, 88.4 percent; college B, 4.2 percent; and college C, 7.5 percent. The effective cost of this $5,000 no-need aid award to college C is $(5,000)(0.075)/(0.075 - 0.010) = \$5,769$ per student per year (exclusive of tuition).

If college C provides a guaranteed renewable, full-cost scholarship of $10,000 (i.e., reduces its cost to $0 for four years), the choice probabilities shift to: college A, 59.0 percent; college B, 2.8 percent; and college C, 38.2 percent. This would represent an effective cost of $(10,000)(0.382)/(0.382 - 0.010) = \$10,269$ per student per year, exclusive of tuition. (Note that this last example, with $10,000 of no-need aid, is somewhat speculative, as a grant of $10,000 would be an extreme data point based on our sample data, and we can't have a lot of confidence that the model estimates are highly accurate at such extremes.)

College C is unlikely to attract students in the choice situation described here under any conditions. However, there is very little risk of giving money to students who are going to attend anyway. Thus, the incremental cost per student for the small proportion of students induced to enroll is not much more than the actual value of the scholarship. However, to use this result in practice, college C would need a way to target its half- or full-cost grants to students with choices like the one illustrated here. Also, even though college C would not pay much more than the actual scholarship cost per incremental student (assuming it could find some way to target aid to unlikely prospects), presumably it cannot give very large no-need scholarships to substantial numbers of students.

Alternatively, of course, college C might attempt to improve the quality of its college (e.g., improve faculty and academic facilities), which might ultimately serve to attract a more able student body (see the results in Chapters 6 and 7 for analysis of the factors which influence prior preference). Rather than use no-need aid, a college could invest an equivalent amount in improving the rest of its academic enterprise.

Conclusions

The purpose of this chapter was to estimate a statistical model of the college choice decision-making process. Using the multinomial logit model, we developed and estimated such a model. The main results of this exercise are a set of estimated relative-importance weights that indicate how our high-ability students weighed the various factors at work in the college choice decision.

Our findings indicate that college choice for our high-ability high school students is a complicated decision process. Many factors are weighed and considered. There is no single way to describe the relative importances which students employ in college choice decision-making; many things matter. A concise summary of these findings might be that *students choose colleges primarily on the basis of their prior preferences, and that aid plays a role in the choice process, especially guaranteed renewable scholarship aid.*

The estimated relative-importance weights seem remarkably stable and consistent across a range of demographic variables and choice situations. There appear to be no systematic differences in these weights based on average SAT scores, gender, planned educational level, and planned major field of study, although some dif-ferences based on parental income levels are observed. Also, the concentration of top-tier private schools in students' choice sets does not seem to systematically influence the choice weights.

The following specific conclusions that may be drawn from the findings reported in this chapter:
- Prior preference is the primary determinant of college choice behavior.
- Financial considerations are relevant, but are of secondary importance to prior preference.
- Scholarships are viewed positively by students; other aid (loans and part-time jobs) are viewed neither positively nor negatively by students.
- Institutional costs detract from the overall attractiveness of a college. This effect becomes less important to students as their income increases.
- "Buying" students with no-need aid is possible but costly. It is especially difficult to change students' decisions when they begin with a prior preference for another college alternative.
- Students implicitly penalize a college if they are considerably more academically able than the average student at the college. Students prefer to attend colleges where the students are, on average, fairly close to their own level of ability. This choice factor operates primarily for high income students.
- Renewability of aid is important to students. Students implicitly penalize a college awarding nonrenewable aid by downgrading the amount of the aid. Of course, receiving nonrenewable aid is preferred to receiving no aid at all. This implicit discounting is especially evident for low-income and, to a lesser extent, medium-income students.

Given the importance of prior preference status, Chapter 6 investigates in detail the determinants of prior preference. Details about the financial aid awarding behavior of colleges will be analyzed in Chapter 5.

5. Determinants of financial aid awards

Findings presented in the preceding chapter estimate the influence of monetary factors (college costs and financial aid) on the college choices of high-ability students. This chapter is concerned with the criteria used by colleges in allocating financial aid. To what degree is financial aid based on considerations of academic merit rather than on financial need? Evidence from prior research concerning colleges' use of criteria other than need in allocating aid, and evidence drawn from data in this study, are summarized below.

Background

Venti, in a chapter in Manski and Wise (1983), estimated the relative influences of a number of student and college characteristics in accounting for allocation of discretionary grant aid by the colleges attended by students in the 1972 National Longitudinal Study. Based on his findings, Venti concluded that "variables measuring need (particularly income and tuition) and variables related to merit (particularly class rank and SAT) are of roughly equal importance in determining aid offers" (p. 103). This conclusion was based on simulated changes in aid as indicated by a mathematical model fit to the NLS data. Venti estimated, for example, that differences of ap-

proximately two standard deviations in total SAT scores (360 points), in parents' income ($11,640), and in college tuition (about $1,650) would result in the following changes in aid dollars for students enrolled in four-year colleges: student SAT, $810; parents' income, − $876; and, college tuition, $965.

Further information concerning use of merit criteria in awarding aid and trends over the ten-year period 1974–84 can be obtained from a series of surveys of institutional financial aid practices. Relevant surveys include (1) a 1974 survey by Huff published in the *College Board Review* in 1975 (Huff 1975); (2) a 1977 survey concerned specifically with no-need aid awards (Sidar and Potter 1978); (3) a 1979 survey of admissions policies and practices conducted by the College Board and the American Association of Collegiate Registrars and Admissions Officers, which included questions relating to no-need aid awards (College Board/AACRAO 1980); (4) a 1982 survey concerning institutional use of no-need aid (Porter and McColloch 1982); and (5) a 1984 survey of undergraduate need-analysis policies, practices, and procedures conducted by the College Board and the National Association of Student Financial Aid Administrators (College Board/ NASFAA 1984).

Although differences in populations of institutions surveyed and in definitions of no-need financial aid make the findings of these surveys difficult to compare, the results show a generally

Table 5.1. Summary of published research on use of no-need awards in aid decisions

	Responding four-year institutions reporting use of no-need criteria in awarding aid (%)	
	Public	Private
Huff–1974	54	55
Sidar and Potter–1977	64	74
College Board/AACRAO–1979	60	61
College Board/NASFAA–1984	90	85

consistent pattern of a high and increasing incidence of use of no-need aid awards (see Table 5.1 for a summary of the key findings with regard to the incidence of no-need awarding).

Sidar and Potter (1978) included tuition remissions for children of a college's faculty and staff members in their definition of no-need aid, which may account in part for the higher incidence reported in their study than in other surveys taken at a similar time.

The 1982 Porter and McColloch study does not provide directly comparable figures. However, 25 percent of institutions responding to this survey reported providing financial recognition for academic excellence to 1 percent or less of freshmen. This implies a lower bound estimate of 75 percent of four-year institutions giving no-need aid in 1982, a result consistent with the trends shown in Table 5.1. Several features of no-need aid reported by institutions responding to the 1984 College Board/NASFAA survey are summarized in Table 5.2.

Results of these surveys of college concerning aid policies and practices confirm informal reports and the perceptions of admissions and financial aid officers that increasing numbers of institutions award a portion of financial aid to students on the basis of academic criteria. According to the College Board/NASFAA study,

many of the awards are less than $1,000—an estimated 80 percent at four-year public institutions and an estimated 50 percent at four-year private schools. However, some awards are appreciably larger. Four-year private colleges report that 20 percent of their no-need scholarships exceed $2,000 and 6 percent exceed $4,000.

Incidence and magnitude of aid offers to students in this study

The 1,183 students with whom telephone interviews were completed in our study received 3,988 admissions offers. Of the 1,183 students, 754 (64 percent) were offered financial aid by at least one college. Of the total 3,988 admissions offers, 1,486 (37 percent) were accompanied by offers of financial aid. The average total aid package (including grant, loan, and job aid) was $4,810, a high figure reflecting the fact that a substantial number of admissions and aid offers to students in our sample were from high-cost institutions. The average college cost for colleges making the 1,486 aid offers was $11,062.

The breakdown of aid offers to students in our sample among grant, loan, and job aid is shown

Table 5.2. No-need aid characteristics

	Four-year public	Four-year private
Average number of awards	241	104
Average value of awards	$835	$1,558
Percent renewable	45%	72%
Distribution of awards:		
under $500	35%	13%
$ 500–$1,000	45	37
$1,000–$2,000	17	29
$2,000–$3,000	1	11
$3,000–$4,000	1	3
$4,000 or more	1	6
	100%	100%

Table 5.3. Some financial aid statistics

Type of aid award	Percentage of financial aid offers that included such aid	Average financial aid award
Grant aid	91.4	$3,674
Loan aid	45.1	$2,081
Part-time work aid	36.2	$1,125

Renewability of financial aid offers

Possibility of aid being renewed	Percentage
No response	11.0
No possibility	4.8
Possible	18.9
Probable	54.9
Definite	10.3
	100.0%

Note: The "average financial aid award" numbers refer to all those awards greater than $0.

in Table 5.3, as is reported renewability of financial aid offers. Most students who received college-specific financial aid reported that the likelihood of its renewal was "probable" (54.9 percent) or "definite" (10.3 percent). Only 4.8 percent reported that specific aid offers had "no possibility" of renewal.

These high-ability high school students received considerable amounts of portable financial aid from such sources as state scholarship programs, ROTC, National Merit, and other private scholarship programs. Such portable financial aid is defined to be scholarships awarded to the student by noncollege sources, which may be used by a student at any college of his or her choosing. Some relevant descriptive statistics regarding portable financial aid are displayed in Table 5.4. Almost half (49.0 percent) our students report some portable financial aid. The predominant source of this aid is the National Merit Scholarship Corporation (32.1 percent). Those students

with portable financial aid reported an average amount of $1,229. About half this personal financial aid is not renewable (50.6 percent).

Determinants of aid offers

In response to interview questions concerning no-need aid, a total of 572 students—48 percent of all students interviewed and 76 percent of those offered any aid—stated that one or more colleges had offered aid based in whole or in part on ac-

Table 5.4. Portable financial aid award statistics

Incidence of portable aid

Students with portable aid	49.0%
Students with no portable aid	51.0
	100.0%

Sources of portable financial aid awards

National Merit Scholarship	32.1%
Community organization	18.1
Regents	11.1
Corporation	11.1
State government	6.3
ROTC	3.8
Corporate merit scholarship	3.1
National Honor	0.9
Labor union	0.6
Other	12.4
	100.0%

Amounts of portable financial aid awards

Average	=	$ 1,229
Minimum	=	$ 25
Maximum	=	$11,000

Possibility of renewal of portable financial aid awards

Don't know	1.5%
None	50.6
Possible	6.9
Probable	23.1
Guaranteed	17.0
	100.0%

ademic considerations. This high level of reporting by a sample of academically able students of aid offers based on academic criteria is not surprising in light of the information on institutional practices summarized at the beginning of this chapter.

Institutions' use of other than need-based criteria in awarding financial aid was also evident in the extent to which students reported receiving aid offers from colleges to which they had not applied for financial aid. Table 5.5 shows (for the 3,988 admissions offers) the incidence of aid awards to (a) students applying for aid and (b) students not applying for aid at the college offering admission. Naturally, aid is offered more often to those who apply for it. However, the fact that 14 percent of the offers of admissions to students not applying for aid included aid awards provides further evidence concerning the extent that no-need criteria are used in awarding aid.

Apart from data on college admissions and aid offers, information was available for many students in the study sample concerning family financial circumstances, academic ability, and other variables expected to have a relationship to the incidence and magnitude of financial aid offers. Relevant data on colleges making admissions and aid offers (such as information on college costs) was also available. These data allowed us to examine statistically the extent to which need and merit criteria account for aid awards reported to us by students.

In carrying out these analyses, it was judged important to examine separately certain groups of colleges for which there were *a priori* reasons to expect need and merit criteria to be differentially weighted in aid decisions. A number of the most highly selective colleges in the United States have stated policies of awarding aid on the basis of need only, with exceptions in certain of these colleges for a small number of special scholarships. No-need scholarships were expected to be used more frequently by colleges below the highest levels of academic reputation. A smaller proportion of these colleges subscribe to policies calling for allocation of financial aid on the basis of need only. Furthermore, colleges below the highest levels of academic reputation are expected to use financial incentives more frequently in competing with the most selective colleges for highly able students.

In studying determinants of aid awards, we divided colleges named by students into three groups, using a proxy measure of academic reputation identified for purposes of this study as the AQSCORE (see Chapter 7 for a discussion of the development of this index and its components). The high AQSCORE group consisted of colleges with AQSCOREs higher than one standard deviation above the mean of this index; the middle group consisted of colleges with AQSCOREs between the mean and one standard deviation above the mean and the low group consisted of those colleges with AQSCOREs below the mean. The numbers and percentages of colleges in each group, and the percentages of all admissions offers to students in the sample made by colleges in each group are shown in Table 5.6.

Table 5.5. Incidence of aid awards

| | Applied for aid | | Did not apply for aid | | Total | |
	Number	Percentage	Number	Percentage	Number	Percentage
Aid offered	1,251	54	235	14	1,486	37
Aid not offered	1,078	46	1,424	86	2,502	63
Total	2,329	100	1,659	100	3,988	100

Table 5.6. Colleges' admissions offers by academic reputation group

	Number of colleges	Percentage of colleges	Percentage of admissions offers
High AQSCORE group	83	15%	50%
Middle AQSCORE group	186	34	32
Low AQSCORE group	281	51	18
		100%	100%

The high percentage of admissions offers by the high AQSCORE group (which contains the most highly selective colleges) reflects the fact that this group of colleges received, on average, far more applications from students in our sample than did colleges in the other groups. This is a further indication of the relative attractiveness of such colleges to students like those in our sample.

The relationships of aid offers to student and college characteristics were studied separately for students applying for aid and for those not applying for aid to colleges within each of these three college groups. That is, each admissions offer was assigned to one of six groups:

High AQSCORE group, aid applied for
Middle AQSCORE group, aid applied for
Low AQSCORE group, aid applied for

High AQSCORE group, aid not applied for
Middle AQSCORE group, aid not applied for
Low AQSCORE group, aid not applied for

Within each group, the probability that an admissions offer would be accompanied by an aid offer was examined as a function of (1) student financial need as measured by college costs and expected family contribution and (2) academic ability as measured by SAT scores. Since the dependent variable for this analysis was dichotomous (1 if aid was offered, 0 if aid was not offered), logistic regression methods were used.

Direct measures of expected family contribution to college costs were available for students who had filed with the College Scholarship Service (CSS). Of the total 3,988 admission offers, more than 2,400 involved students with CSS-computed family contributions—primarily students applying for aid at one or more colleges. We also had available from response to the Student Descriptive Questionnaire (SDQ) student-reported information on several key variables included in the CSS computation: family income, parents' number of dependents, and number of other dependents in college during the student's first year. Regression analyses of CSS-contribution figures on these SDQ responses (or functions of these responses) allowed development of a weighted index for imputing family contributions from such responses. The correlation of values of this weighted index with CSS figures was 0.65. Of the 3,988 admission offers, 3,478 were to students for whom family contributions could be imputed. Because the incidence of financial aid awards was to be studied both for aid applicants and for students not applying for aid, family contributions imputed from SDQ responses (rather than CSS figures) were used throughout in the modeling of aid award incidence.

Table 5.7 gives the estimated parameters of the logistic regression models for aid incidence for aid applicants and for aid non-applicants in each of the three college groups. Generally the findings conform to prior expectations.

Aid applicants

For aid applicants in the high AQSCORE group, the effects of college costs and imputed family contribution are large and statistically significant.

Table 5.7. Estimated parameters of logistic regression models for aid incidence (offered vs. not-offered financial aid)

| | College quality groups | | | | | |
| | High AQSCORE group | | Middle AQSCORE group | | Low AQSCORE group | |
	Coefficient	T-Ratio	Coefficient	T-Ratio	Coefficient	T-Ratio
Aid applicants						
College costs (in $000s)	0.0652	2.75*	0.1610	6.60*	0.1805	4.55*
Imputed family contribution (in $000s)	−0.1590	−9.92*	−0.0505	−2.76*	−0.0249	−1.08
Average SAT score (V and M)	0.0013	1.01	0.0057	4.41*	0.0053	3.12*
Constant term	0.0739		−4.8037		−4.3446	
Non–aid applicants						
College costs (in $000s)	−0.1512	−4.48*	0.0280	0.72	0.1060	1.98
Imputed family contribution (in $000s)	0.0240	0.71	−0.0730	−2.71*	−0.0435	−1.39
Average SAT score (V and M)	0.0133	4.12*	0.0070	3.55*	0.0119	4.19*
Constant term	−10.3641		−5.8152		−9.0969	

Note: An asterisk denotes coefficients that are statistically significant at the 1 percent level.

The coefficient for SAT scores is positive, but it is small and not statistically significant. Need criteria are clearly predominant in accounting for incidence of aid awards to aid applicants in this group.

For aid applicants in the middle AQSCORE group, the effects of college costs and imputed family contribution are statistically significant, though family contribution has a weaker effect than in the high AQSCORE group. In this group, the effect of SAT scores on incidence of aid offers is large and statistically significant.

For aid applicants to colleges in the low AQSCORE group, college costs and SAT scores have large and statistically significant effects. The sign of the coefficient for imputed family contribution is in the expected negative direction (students from families with higher expected contributions are less likely to be offered aid), but the coefficient is small in absolute value and is not statistically significant.

In summary, different factors account for the probabilities of aid awards from colleges in the three groups to aid applicants in our sample. In the high AQSCORE group, need-based criteria predominate. In the middle group, need and merit criteria are both important. In the low group, academic ability is important, and imputed family contribution has a small effect on the probability of an aid offer.

It should be noted that these findings apply only to students like those in the population we sampled from—in particular, students with average SAT scores of 550 and above. Such students have academic credentials that are far stronger than those presented by most applicants to many nonselective colleges. Although imputed family contribution does not discriminate well between aid applicants in our sample who were and were not offered aid by colleges in the low AQSCORE group, it might well have a stronger effect on incidence of aid offers to the larger population of admitted students in these colleges.

Non–aid applicants

For students not applying for aid, SAT scores had a strong and statistically significant positive effect on the probability that a student would be offered aid within each of the three college groups. Clearly, aid offers to non–aid applicants are largely predicated on evidence of academic ability.

College costs had a statistically significant *negative* effect in the high AQSCORE group on probability that nonapplicants would be offered aid, in contrast to the observation for aid applicants that the probability of aid increased (as expected) with increasing college costs. This finding suggests that the practice of offering aid to students not applying for it is more common among relatively low-cost colleges within the high AQSCORE group.

Imputed family contribution had a statistically significant negative effect on the probability of an aid award to a student not applying for aid for colleges in the middle AQSCORE group. It appears that these colleges use both need and academic criteria in deciding to offer aid awards to non–aid applicants. Perhaps this form of aid is targeted to able students from families judged to have a relatively high degree of difficulty in meeting college costs and who might therefore be more responsive to differences in net college costs produced by aid offers.

While colleges in all three groups offered aid to students who had not applied for it, and while academic criteria appeared to be used predominantly in allocating these awards, there were strong differences among the three college groups in the extent to which aid was offered to nonapplicants. To illustrate, the models for aid incidence provide the following estimates of probabilities that a non–aid applicant with an imputed contribution of $10,000 and average SAT scores of 650 will be offered aid by colleges with costs of $10,000 in each of the three groups: 0.05 in the high AQSCORE group, 0.15 in the middle AQSCORE group, and 0.32 in the low AQSCORE group.

Table 5.8 provides illustrative estimates of probabilities that aid applicants and nonapplicants with certain combinations of SAT scores and imputed family contributions will be offered aid at colleges in each of the three groups. For these illustrations, college costs have been held constant at an assumed total cost of $10,000. The values calculated in these illustrations should not be taken as precise estimates of the actual probabilities that students with the given SAT scores and family contribution values will be offered aid at any given college. The estimates are different than they would have been had actual CSS contribution figures (rather than an index correlated with the CSS values) been used in the analyses, and they were derived by aggregating across colleges. Furthermore, they cannot account for adjustments individual colleges may make in need calculations. These illustrations are presented primarily to highlight relative changes in aid probabilities in response to SAT and family contribution differences for aid applicants and nonapplicants in the three college groups.

	Imputed contribution	Aid applicants' SAT scores			Non–aid applicants' SAT scores		
		550	650	750	550	650	750
High AQSCORE group							
Low	($ 1,000)	.78	.80	.82	.01	.04	.13
Medium	($ 5,000)	.66	.68	.71	.01	.04	.14
High	($10,000)	.46	.50	.53	.01	.05	.16
Middle AQSCORE group							
Low	($ 1,000)	.47	.61	.74	.15	.26	.41
Medium	($ 5,000)	.42	.56	.70	.11	.21	.34
High	($10,000)	.36	.50	.64	.08	.15	.26
Low AQSCORE group							
Low	($ 1,000)	.59	.71	.80	.18	.41	.70
Medium	($ 5,000)	.56	.69	.79	.15	.37	.66
High	($10,000)	.53	.66	.77	.13	.32	.61

Table 5.9 shows the changes in aid probabilities implied by each of the six models that are associated with the following differences in imputed family contribution and in SAT scores:
1. A reduction in contribution from $10,000 to $1,000 (holding SAT scores constant at 650 and college costs constant at $10,000), and
2. An increase in SAT scores from 550 to 750 (holding the contribution constant at $5,000 and college costs constant at $10,000).

These differences provide specific illustrations of certain of the main conclusions just summarized. It is clear that relatively large changes in aid probabilities are associated with differences in estimated family contributions for aid applicants to colleges in the high AQSCORE group. Such changes are also associated with differences in SAT scores for both aid applicants and nonapplicants in the middle and low AQSCORE groups. All other differences in this illustration are small in practical terms.

Aid amounts in excess of calculated need

The preceding section focused on incidence of aid offers without respect to the amounts of aid offered. In this section, we discuss the results of analyses comparing total aid offers to calculated financial "need." For this purpose, calculated need was taken to be the difference between total college costs and the CSS estimate of expected family contribution toward these costs. (For these analyses, it was deemed important to use the actual CSS figures rather than imputed values, and the analyses therefore are limited to CSS filers.) If the difference between the total dollar amount of an aid offer and the need calculated as previously defined was positive, the offer was considered to exceed need. If this difference was zero or negative (or if no aid was offered), the case was classified as one in which aid did not exceed need.

Table 5.9. Illustrative changes in aid probabilities

| | Estimated change in aid probability associated with | |
	Contribution difference	SAT difference
Aid applicants		
High AQSCORE group	.30	.05
Middle AQSCORE group	.11	.28
Low AQSCORE group	.05	.23
Non–aid applicants		
High AQSCORE group	− .01	.13
Middle AQSCORE group	.11	.23
Low AQSCORE group	.09	.51

Even if colleges awarded aid based only on financial need, we would not expect aid figures to match precisely our calculated need figures for all students. Apart from possible errors in our financial aid data for some students, discrepancies would arise from the fact that colleges adjust the CSS figures in forming their own estimates of need and from the fact that different total expense budgets may be appropriate for different students. For these reasons, we will focus attention on patterns in the data (rather than on absolute differences) and on the degree to which aid exceeding "need" is related to other variables.

Table 5.10 shows by AQSCORE group and by interval on SAT score the number of admissions offers to CSS filers, the percent of these accompanied by aid offers greater than calculated need, and the distribution of this "excess aid" in dollars over several intervals. Within each college group, the percentage of offers in excess of need clearly tends to increase with increasing SAT scores. (Curiously, however, students in the 650–699 and 700–749 SAT intervals have about the same percentage of offers in excess of need within each college group.) To illustrate the range of differ-

ences, the following chart contrasts the percentages of students in the lowest and highest SAT intervals offered excess aid by colleges in each of the three groups.

| | SAT score interval | |
	550–599	750–800
High AQSCORE group	4	25
Middle AQSCORE group	13	33
Low AQSCORE group	17	46

Holding SAT score interval constant, percentages of excess awards also increase as one moves from the high to the middle to the low AQSCORE group. Consistent with the findings on aid incidence described above, these results suggest that colleges in lower AQSCORE groups weight academic criteria more heavily than those in higher groups in determining amounts of financial aid awards.

While Table 5.10 presents results descriptively, it should be noted that the effects of college group and SAT score interval were tested formally in log-linear analyses. Likelihood-ratio tests indicated that both these factors and their interaction were statistically necessary (at levels of significance beyond 0.0001) to account for cell frequencies in the table.

Despite the differences among college groups when SAT scores are held constant, it is worthy of note that the overall percentages of awards in excess of need to students in our sample without respect to SAT scores are similar for the three groups, ranging from 21 percent to 25 percent. This similarity arises because the colleges in the higher groups have proportionately larger numbers of admitted students in the higher SAT intervals where excess aid offers are relatively more frequent. From this perspective, it could be argued that the evidence suggests that colleges in the three groups respond somewhat similarly to academic criteria in determining aid offers in excess of need, but that this responsivenes is a

Table 5.10. Percentages of aid offers exceeding calculated need

	Number of admissions offers	Percentage with aid offers above calculated need	Percentage with offers exceeding need by:			
			$1–$1,000	$1,001–$2,000	$2,001–$3,000	$3,000 +
High AQSCORE group						
550–599	48	4	0	2	0	2
600–649	132	15	7	2	3	3
650–699	211	19	9	4	2	4
700–749	325	18	9	2	4	3
750–800	461	25	5	5	5	10
Total	1,177	21	7	4	4	6
Middle AQSCORE group						
550–599	144	13	4	5	1	3
600–649	173	15	7	2	3	3
650–699	173	25	12	5	3	5
700–749	156	22	10	3	5	4
750–800	153	33	10	8	5	10
Total	799	22	9	5	3	5
Low AQSCORE group						
550–599	142	17	8	5	2	2
600–649	117	22	10	3	3	6
650–699	82	31	16	9	1	5
700–749	53	29	9	8	8	4
750–800	48	46	17	10	13	6
Total	442	25	11	6	4	4

function of the academic ability of a student *relative to* the distribution of academic ability in the pool of admitted students. Students with SAT scores of 750–800 accepted to colleges in the high AQSCORE group, students with scores of 650–699 accepted to colleges in the middle group, and those with scores of 600–649 accepted to colleges in the low group have similar chances of being offered aid in excess of calculated need. Although these students differ in absolute SAT scores, their relative standings in the pools of admitted students in each college group are no doubt more similar.

The results summarized in Table 5.10 also suggest that for the high and middle college groups, particularly high awards are offered relatively frequently to students in the highest SAT interval (750–800). For both of these groups, 10 percent of CSS filers with scores in this interval reported aid awards exceeding calculated need by more than $3,000. This finding may reflect the practice of certain colleges in these groups of awarding large merit scholarships (some equal to full tuition) to small numbers of students with very strong academic credentials.

Summary

Our findings relating to the determinants of financial aid awards are highly consistent with other information and institutional self-reports concerning policies on the allocation of financial aid.

Colleges at the highest levels of academic reputation appear to rely primarily on information concerning student financial need in deciding whether to offer financial aid to students who have applied for it. However, it is evident that some colleges in the highest group defined for this study (generally lower-cost colleges within this group) make aid offers to students with strong academic credentials who have not applied for aid. It is also evident that even in this highest group, increases in SAT scores are associated with greater probabilities that students will be offered aid exceeding calculated financial need.

In general, colleges ranked lower on an index of academic reputation are far more responsive to students' academic ability than are higher-ranked colleges in determining financial aid awards. Strikingly, in the lower two college groups defined for this study, the probability a student would be offered aid varied by only a small amount in response to large changes in imputed family contribution to college costs, while this probability varied by much larger amounts in response to increases from 550 to 750 on the SAT. Moreover, the percentages of students receiving aid offers in excess of need from colleges in these groups increase sharply with increasing SAT scores.

6. Antecedents of college choice behavior: Preference judgment formation

Preference judgment formation, the immediate antecedent of choice behavior, is analyzed in this chapter. An antecedent of both choice behavior and preference judgment formation—perception judgment formation—will be analyzed in Chapter 7. Given the results in Chapter 4, prior preference is of crucial importance in explaining college choice behavior. We seek to examine and analyze the determinants of prior preference formation in this chapter. In our multistage college choice model, prior preference is postulated to depend on a student's perceptions of the college alternatives.

Development of perceptual ratings indices

To describe college alternatives in terms of students' perceptions, we construct composite perceptual ratings indices. Factor analysis procedures are used to assess the underlying correlation pattern in our perceptual ratings scales. Then, four key composite perceptual ratings indices are developed. The details of this index construction are described in this section.

Definitions of the 14 raw perceptual ratings used in this study are displayed in Table 6.1. These definitions are the actual phrases used in the survey research questionnaires. The 14 scales were developed with reference to previous research on the determinants of college choice behavior. The main sources consulted were Astin, et al. (1983, 1984, and 1985), Chapman (1977, 1979), Kohn, Manski, and Mundel (1976), Litten et al. (1983), and Manski and Wise (1983).

These 14 perceptual ratings were collected on the following grading scale: A = "excellent"; B = "good"; C = "fair"; D = "poor"; and, F = "unacceptable." For analysis purposes, these letter grades were transformed into a 1–5 numerical scale, where 1 = "F" and 5 = "A."

These 14 perceptual ratings of each college presumably represent fewer than 14 completely separate and distinct aspects of colleges. Even though an attempt was made to have them represent relatively distinct dimensions on college features, correlation among the ratings is inevitable, if for no other reason than the presence of cross-scale halo effects. Thus, it is appropriate to seek a reduced-space representation of these perceptual ratings scales.

Standardization transformations

In seeking to construct a perceptual space to describe the perceived positioning of colleges, a number of issues of data scaling arise with regard to the college ratings provided by the survey re-

Table 6.1. Definitions of perceptual ratings used in this study

Variable	Definition
DIVERSITY	Academic diversity (range of courses offered)
FACILITIES	Academic facilities (library, computer resources, laboratories, etc.)
GEOLOCATE	Geographical location (part of the country, distance from home)
REPUTATION	Overall academic reputation
LOWCOST	Low overall costs (tuition, fees, room and board, other expenses)
SOCIALFIT	Social climate (college atmosphere, what the student body is like, how you would fit in)
SPECPROG	Availability of special majors, degrees, or honors programs
COMMUNITY	Community setting (urban, suburban, small town, rural)
PREPGRAD	Preparation for career or graduate and professional school opportunities
AIDAVAIL	Availability of financial aid
CONTACT	Personal contact with college representatives (admissions staff, faculty, coaches, others)
ACADSTRN	Academic strength in your major areas of interest
UGRADEMP	Emphasis on undergraduate education (small classes, faculty contact, etc.)
EXTRACUR	Opportunities for involvement in extra-curricular activities (clubs, sports, performing arts, journalism, etc.)

spondents. These issues concern ratings variability across attributes and respondents (see Dillon, Frederick, and Tangpanichdee 1985 for a review of these issues).

The specific scaling adopted here follows the suggestion of Dillon, Frederick, and Tangpanichdee (1985, pp. 57–58). In particular, the raw ratings data were standardized to highlight the within-respondent variance on the attribute ratings over the colleges rated by each respondent. Each attribute was standardized (to mean zero and variance one) across the colleges rated for each respondent separately. That is, the ratings on the first attribute for the first respondent over that respondent's colleges were transformed to have mean zero and variance one. This procedure was repeated for the second and subsequent attributes of the first respondent, ultimately resulting in all the ratings data for the respondent being standardized to mean zero and variance one for each attribute. This procedure was then repeated for all respondents. As summarized by Dillon, Frederick, and Tangpanichdee: "The standardi-

zations within each respondent will remove from the analysis the variance on the attribute characteristics due to individual level effects. The remaining variance gives the interrelationships between changes in the attribute characteristics over the brands generalized across the respondents."

Redundancy structure among the perceptual ratings

The correlations in the standardized perceptual ratings are displayed in Table 6.2. The correlations between the various perceptual ratings scales may be noted to be relatively modest. There are only a few values greater than 0.35 in absolute value. Still, further analysis is necessary to determine whether it is possible to represent these 14 perceptual ratings in a more compact, simpler fashion.

In an attempt to reduce these 14 perceptual ratings to a more manageable and interpretable number, a principal components factor analysis was conducted. The results of the varimax rota-

Table 6.2. Correlations among the 14 (standardized) perceptual ratings scales

No.	Variable	2	3	4	5	6	7	8	9	10	11	12	13	14
1	DIVERSITY	36	00	17	−08	06	34	04	19	−04	−15	20	−23	20
2	FACILITIES		00	34	−20	−02	31	05	32	−01	−07	31	−13	10
3	GEOLOCATE			−01	06	17	−04	31	−01	00	02	01	02	10
4	REPUTATION				−41	01	21	08	44	−06	01	33	11	06
5	LOWCOST					10	−17	−04	−24	17	−02	−17	−09	−04
6	SOCIALFIT						01	25	01	09	20	05	16	25
7	SPECPROG							03	32	02	01	31	−06	06
8	COMMUNITY								07	03	09	04	06	13
9	PREPGRAD									02	05	39	05	08
10	AIDAVAIL										20	00	14	10
11	CONTACT											02	38	15
12	ACADSTRN												−01	06
13	UGRADEMP													07
14	EXTRACUR													

Note: These correlations are rescaled into the −100 to +100 interval for presentation purposes. Thus, a reported correlation of 40 represents a Pearson Product Moment Correlation of 0.40.

The correlations were calculated for all nonmissing pairs of variables. The sample sizes for the individual ratings varied from 3,139 to 3,255.

Table 6.3. Results of the varimax rotation of the five-factor solution of the 14 perceptual ratings

Variable	Factors					Communality
	1	2	3	4	5	
DIVERSITY			0.501			0.644
FACILITIES	0.639					0.490
GEOLOCATE				0.798		0.643
REPUTATION	0.597					0.615
LOWCOST					0.730	0.659
SOCIALFIT			0.530			0.511
SPECPROG	0.641					0.461
COMMUNITY				0.761		0.608
PREPGRAD	0.722					0.563
AIDAVAIL					0.702	0.645
CONTACT		0.725				0.581
ACADSTRN	0.692					0.488
UGRADEMP		0.791				0.637
EXTRACUR			0.823			0.697

Note: Only factor loadings with values of 0.50 or greater in absolute value are displayed in this table.

tion for the five-factor solution are displayed in Table 6.3. These five factors, which account for 58.9 percent of the variance in the original 14 perceptual ratings, may be described as: academic quality (ACADQUALITY), quality of personal contact and "personalness" of the college (PERSONALNESS), nonacademic lifestyle considerations (LIFESTYLE), locational considerations (LOCATION), and financial considerations (MONEY). The five-factor solution communalities for these 14 perceptual ratings variables range from 0.46 to 0.70. Thus, this five-factor solution represents about one-half to two-thirds of the variation in each of the 14 raw perceptual ratings scale. We conclude that this reduced space representation of the 14 perceptual variables is interpretable and parsimonious, and that it captures the essence of the original 14 raw perceptual ratings variables.

Construction of the composite perceptual ratings indices

Rather than use factor scores (as derived from the factor analysis results previously described) directly as composite indices of college perceptions, we constructed our own indices using these results from this factor analysis as a guide. In particular, we combined the original scales in a simple weighted additive fashion so that interpretation would be facilitated. The weights were the inverse of each standardized rating's standard deviation, so that ratings with more variability would not implicitly dominate the composite indices.

Our composite indices are defined as follows:

where the weights $w_1, w_2, \cdots, w_{14}$ are the inverse of the perceptual rating standard deviations, appropriately rescaled to sum to 1.0 in each of these composite indices for ease of interpretation. These weights are displayed in Table 6.4.

A multinomial logit model of college preference judgment formation

Preference for a college is viewed as depending on perceptual ratings, individual–institution interactions, and college-specific influences. In our model of college choice behavior, preference refers to all things students value in a college *except* situational constraints (including money considerations).

Model formulation

Unconstrained preferences were obtained from the respondents to the mail survey. The students were asked to rank their three highest-preference colleges from among those to which they had applied. To unconstrain these preference judgments, they were specifically instructed to presume that they had free choice among these colleges (they were to assume that they had admissions offers from all colleges) and that cost was not an issue. These rank-ordered preferences served as the dependent variable in the multinomial logit model of preference judgment formation.

The four nonmonetary composite perceptual ratings indices—ACADQUALITY, PERSONALNESS, LIFESTYLE, and LOCATION—for each of

$$ACADQUALITY = w_2 FACILITIES + w_4 REPUTATION + w_7 SPECPROG + w_9 PREPGRAD + w_{12} ACADSTRN$$
$$PERSONALNESS = w_{11} CONTACT + w_{13} UGRADEMP$$
$$LIFESTYLE = w_1 DIVERSITY + w_6 SOCIALFIT + w_{14} EXTRACUR$$
$$LOCATION = w_3 GEOLOCATE + w_8 COMMUNITY$$
$$MONEY = w_5 LOWCOST + w_{10} AIDAVAIL$$

Table 6.4. Weights used in the development of the five composite perceptual ratings indices

No.	Variable	Original standard deviation	Inverse of the standard deviation[1]	Rescaled weights[2]
1	DIVERSITY	0.61	1.65	0.34
2	FACILITIES	0.56	1.77	0.20
3	GEOLOCATE	0.69	1.45	0.49
4	REPUTATION	0.57	1.77	0.20
5	LOWCOST	0.64	1.56	0.48
6	SOCIALFIT	0.68	1.46	0.30
7	SPECPROG	0.59	1.69	0.19
8	COMMUNITY	0.68	1.48	0.51
9	PREPGRAD	0.50	1.99	0.22
10	AIDAVAIL	0.59	1.71	0.52
11	CONTACT	0.68	1.47	0.49
12	ACADSTRN	0.58	1.73	0.19
13	UGRADEMP	0.66	1.51	0.51
14	EXTRACUR	0.56	1.79	0.36

1. For each rating, "inverse of the standard deviation" equals one divided by the "original standard deviation."
2. The "rescaled weights" refer to the rescaling of the inverses of the standard deviation so that the rescaled weights on each of the 5 indices add up to 1.0.

the (up to three) college alternatives served as the main independent variables. In addition, college-specific indicator variables were included for each of the colleges with more than 150 mentions in the mail survey.

These *base model* variables are defined in Table 6.5. They all have straightforward interpretations, except perhaps for the variable MISSING. This variable is included to model out the effects of missing raw perceptual ratings. As with all surveys, there was some item nonresponse to the perceptual ratings questions. That is, some respondents provided perceptual ratings for some but not all of the 12 nonmonetary perceptual ratings. Methods of handling such missing data include deleting it from analysis, adding variable-specific missing-value indicator variables to account for the influence of such values, or assigning a particular value to the missing variables

(such as the mean of the nonmissing values for a variable). Rather than add an extra 12 such variables, or adopt the extreme option of dropping such preference sets from the analysis altogether, a single missing-value variable was added to the model. MISSING equals the number of missing perceptual ratings values. Since the incidence of missing values was small, this single variable should serve to conveniently account for their influence.

Several other individual–institution interaction variables were additional possible candidates for inclusion in our multinomial logit model of college preference judgment formation. Familial ties to a college (whether either parent attended the college) and distance from the campus to the student's residence were viewed as possibly being relevant (see Table 6.6 for definitions of these extra variables). Since our prior beliefs of the

Table 6.5. Definitions of the variables included in the preference judgment formation model

Group/variables	Definition
Perceptual ratings	
ACADQUALITY	Academic quality index (a composite index)
PERSONALNESS	Personalness index (a composite index)
LIFESTYLE	Lifestyle index (a composite index)
LOCATION	Location index (a composite index)
College-specific effects	
COLLEGE1	An indicator variable which equals 1 for the most frequently mentioned college in terms of applications submitted by our 1,549 mail survey respondents, and equals 0 otherwise.
COLLEGE2 through COLLEGE7	Indicator variables for the second through seventh most frequently mentioned colleges in terms of applications submitted by our 1,549 mail survey respondents.
Other variables	
MISSING	The number of missing original perceptual rating values (from 0 to 12).

Table 6.6. Other variables tested in the extended preference judgment formation model

Variable	Definition
FATHER	An indicator variable that equals 1 if a student's father attended a college and equals 0 otherwise.
MOTHER	An indicator variable that equals 1 if a student's mother attended a college and equals 0 otherwise.
DISTANCE	The distance (in 000s of miles) from the campus of a college to the residence of a student.

importance of these variables were less strong than for those in the base model, they were categorized as being candidates for an *extended model*. Specific hypothesis testing would indicate whether they should be included in the model.

Estimation and model-specification analysis

A total of 1,224 students' data from the mail survey were available for analysis. These students had applied to and had ranked at least two colleges, and they had provided the corresponding perceptual ratings data. Of these 1,224 students, 1,181 provided sufficiently complete college ranking (with no ties) and perceptual ratings data to permit their use for estimation purposes.

Maximum-likelihood procedures were used to estimate the parameters (relative-importance weights) of this multinomial logit model. A linear additive functional relationship was assumed. The results of this estimation are displayed in Table 6.7.

Table 6.7. Results of estimating the preference judgment formation model

Variable	Coefficient estimate	Standard error	T-Ratio
ACADQUALITY	1.9869	0.1430	13.894
PERSONALNESS	0.7148	0.0742	9.637
LIFESTYLE	0.8438	0.1069	7.892
LOCATION	0.7124	0.0752	9.479
MISSING	−0.7189	0.3074	−2.339
COLLEGE1	1.2112	0.2004	6.046
COLLEGE2	0.2582	0.2014	1.282
COLLEGE3	0.9460	0.2270	4.167
COLLEGE4	1.0334	0.2071	4.990
COLLEGE5	1.2201	0.2333	5.230
COLLEGE6	0.7261	0.2413	3.010
COLLEGE7	0.5790	0.2620	2.210

Summary statistics
Number of choice sets = 1,181
Initial log-likelihood = −1,181.1
Final log-likelihood = −805.4
Log-likelihood ratio index = 0.318

Note: Refer to the discussion in Appendix 1 for details and interpretations of the various log-likelihood statistics.

Hypothesis tests were performed to assess whether the variables described in Table 6.6 should be included in our base model. With regard to the FATHER and MOTHER variables, the relevant chi-squared test-statistic value was 2.6 (with the corresponding critical chi-squared value of 9.2, for 2 degrees of freedom and a 1 percent level of significance). With regard to DISTANCE, the relevant chi-squared test statistic was 5.0 (with the corresponding critical chi-squared value of 6.6, for 1 degree of freedom and a 1 percent level of significance). In both cases, then, the results suggest that these variables do not contribute significantly, given the presence of the other variables in the model. Thus, on the grounds of parsimony, we chose not to include FATHER, MOTHER, and DISTANCE in the preference judgment formation model.

The results reported in Table 6.7 are for an explosion depth of one. As in the case of the choice model described in Chapter 4, only the first-choice prior preference data could be used to estimate the preference model's parameters. Attempts to exploit the rank-ordered nature of the prior preference data, as described in Chapman and Staelin (1982), were unsuccessful. In testing whether the second prior preference ranking could be used, the conclusion was that explosion to a depth of two was not appropriate for these data. The relevant chi-squared test-statistic value was 29.6 (with the corresponding critical chi-squared value of 26.2, for 12 degrees of freedom and a 1 percent level of significance). Thus, we reject the null hypothesis that the first- and second-ranked prior preference choice observations yield equivalent relative-importance weights in this preference judgment formation model.

Interpretation of the preference judgment formation results

All variables (except one of the college-specific effects) in our preference judgment formation model are statistically significant at the 5 percent level, and most are statistically significant at well beyond the 1 percent level. The LLRI value of 0.318 is toward the high end of the range of LLRI values for comparable college choice studies (see Table A1.1 in Appendix 1 for LLRI values for other college choice studies. Of course, we are modeling prior preference here, not final college choice). We conclude from this that our model performs well, in a statistical goodness-of-fit sense, in accounting for the determinants of preference judgment formation.

In forming preferences, the most important perceptual dimension is academic quality (ACAD-QUALITY). These results are consistent with other studies, such as Kohn, Manski, and Mundel (1976), Chapman (1977, 1979), Punj and Staelin (1978), and Manski and Wise (1983) where objective measures of college quality were found to be the most important determinant of college choice.

PERSONALNESS, LIFESTYLE, and LOCATION are all important considerations to students when they form prior preference judgments about colleges. In fact, their impact on prior preference is approximately equal, with relative-importance weights (coefficients) of 0.7148, 0.8438, and 0.7124, respectively. Their influence on prior preference is positive: holding other factors constant, increases in perceived PERSONALNESS, LIFESTYLE, and LOCATION improve the prior preference probabilities. However, the partial effect of each of these variables individually is less than one-half of that of ACADQUALITY.

In interpreting the college-specific effects, it is important to note that they represent the incremental impact of a college after accounting for the perceptual ratings. Thus, if the perceptual ratings had fully captured all the relevant dimensions, these indicator variables would not have been necessary. Six of the seven college-specific effects are statistically significant at the 5 percent level; all are positive. Holding other factors constant, being a top-seven college improves the prior preference probability by a positive amount, above and beyond that conferred by the perceptual ratings indices.

MISSING is negative and significant (at a 5 percent level). Since it models out missing data on any of the underlying 12 perceptual ratings scales, the negative sign is interpreted as missing data being implicitly held against a college.

In responding to the mail questionnaire, students both provided ratings of colleges on the perceptual scales and reported their importance weights for these factors (on a 1-to-4 scale). It is instructive to compare our statistically inferred importance weights (from the multinomial logit analysis described above) with the self-reported importance weights for the factors as provided directly by the students. Some relevant summary statistics for the self-reported importance weights from the mail survey respondents are reported in Table 6.8. Four of the ACADQUALITY ratings scales (FACILITIES, REPUTATION, PREPGRAD, and ACADSTRN) are among the five highest-rated perceptual dimensions on a self-reported basis. Furthermore, if we construct average self-reported values for our composite indices (using the data from Table 6.8), the average self-reported weights are 3.32, 2.70, 3.09, and 2.72, for ACADQUALITY, PERSONALNESS, LIFESTYLE, and LOCATION, respectively. This pattern and its ordering is virtually identical to the coefficient estimates reported in Table 6.6. However, note that the coefficient estimate on ACADQUALITY from the multinomial logit model is more than twice the size of the coefficient estimates on the

Table 6.8. *Self-reported relative-importance weights of perceptual dimensions*

Perceptual dimension	Definition	Summary statistics	
		Mean	Standard deviation
ACADSTRN	Academic strength in area of interest	3.627	0.631
REPUTATION	Reputation	3.613	0.586
DIVERSITY	Academic diversity	3.332	0.743
FACILITIES	Facilities	3.321	0.718
PREPGRAD	Preparation for graduate study/career	3.216	0.841
SOCIALFIT	Social activities	3.122	0.821
UGRADEMP	Emphasis on undergraduate studies	3.017	0.831
GEOLOCATE	Location setting	2.919	0.913
SPECPROG	Special programs	2.842	0.912
EXTRACUR	Extracurricular activities	2.809	0.876
AIDAVAIL	Financial aid availability	2.526	1.126
COMMUNITY	Community setting	2.522	0.909
CONTACT	Contact with admissions personnel	2.388	0.963
LOWCOST	Low cost	2.254	0.997

Note: Self-reported importance weights were reported on a 1–4 scale, where:

4 = very important

3 = important

2 = somewhat important

1 = not important.

These self-reported importance weights are based on 1,549 responses to the mail survey.

three other composite perceptual indices. The self-reported weights appear to understate the differences in importance across the factors. Nonetheless, this overall consistency between statistically derived relative-importance weights and self-reported relative importance weights is noteworthy. Such corroboration from two independent sources serves to reinforce the confidence that we may place in the multinomial logit model weights.

Individual differences analysis

To assess whether students' backgrounds influence their preference weights, we conducted individual differences analyses similar to those conducted for the college choice model. These analyses require the use of statistical-pooling tests to determine, for example, whether the relative-importance weights of men are statistically identical to those of women. The mechanics of these pooling tests for the multinomial logit model are described in Appendix 1.

Demographic variables. We tested for heterogeneity of weights for the following demographic variables (and subgroups of students): average SAT scores ("less than or equal to 675"; "more than 675"), gender ("male"; "female"), planned educational level ("bachelor's or uncertain"; "graduate school"), planned major field of study ("sciences"; "engineering"; "other"), and paren-

Table 6.9. Individual differences analysis: Pooling test results for demographic variables[1]

	Calculated test statistic	Degrees of freedom	Critical value	Conclusion[2]
Average SAT scores (2 groups)	14.4	12	26.2	n/s
Gender (2 groups)	15.6	12	26.2	n/s
Planned educational level (2 groups)	11.6	12	26.2	n/s
Planned major field of study (3 groups)	52.6	24	43.0	Significant
Parental income (3 groups)	35.6	24	43.0	n/s

1. A 1 percent level of statistical significance was used in these tests.
2. Under "Conclusion," "n/s" means that the calculated test-statistic value does not exceed the critical value, so the null hypothesis that the groups have identical relative-importance weights cannot be rejected; "significant" means that the groups apparently are characterized by different relative-importance weights.

tal income level ("$30,000 or less"; "$30,001–$49,999"; "$50,000 or more"). The results of these tests are displayed in Table 6.9.

The pooling test results shown in Table 6.9 indicate that only in the case of major field of study are the relative-importance weights different. Thus, we may conclude that the preference weights reported in Table 6.7 adequately describe all SAT levels (in the range represented in our sample, 550–800), men and women, planned educational levels (bachelor's only versus graduate school intentions), and all income levels. There are no apparent individual differences based on these demographic variables. However, since there are apparently some differences across major field of study groups, a detailed examination of these differences is appropriate.

Major field of study effects. The coefficients for the various major field of study groups are shown in Table 6.10. Major differences across fields of study are described below.

The primary differences across fields of study appear to be college-specific effects. The extra impact of being specific top-seven colleges varies somewhat by the student's field of study. A second notable difference concerns the relative weights on ACADQUALITY and LIFESTYLE. In all field of study groups, ACADQUALITY is the most important consideration. However, LIFE-STYLE appears to be considerably more important to "other" students than it is to engineering and science students. Indeed, while ACADQUAL-ITY is about three times as important as LIFE-STYLE for engineering and science students, it is only about one and one-third times as important as LIFESTYLE for "other" students.

In sum, individual differences exist for students classified by intended field of study, but they appear to be relatively modest in scope. Perceived academic quality is consistently the most important consideration for students in all fields of study.

Table 6.10. Coefficient estimates for different planned major fields of study

Variable	All students with reported major field of study	Students reporting that their major field of study would be:		
		Engineering	Science	"Other"
ACADQUALITY	1.9781**	2.2985**	2.1949**	1.6941**
PERSONALNESS	0.7159**	0.7787**	0.7168**	0.7683**
LIFESTYLE	0.8305**	0.6603**	0.7343**	1.2763**
LOCATION	0.7066**	0.5516**	0.8898**	0.6274**
MISSING	−0.7145*	0.2080	−1.1325*	−0.4800
COLLEGE1	1.2107**	−2.1885	1.7027**	0.9526**
COLLEGE2	0.2456	0.4574	0.3450	0.1069
COLLEGE3	0.9214**	1.0030	1.5198**	0.4874
COLLEGE4	1.0332**	0.8044*	0.8870**	1.7041**
COLLEGE5	1.2438**	1.3137**	1.3291**	−1.2140
COLLEGE6	0.6924**	1.4574	0.5289	0.8207*
COLLEGE7	0.5774*	0.3424	1.0919**	0.1902
Summary statistics				
No. of choice sets	1161	278	492	391
Initial LL	−1170.5	−280.7	−498.7	−391.0
Final LL	−798.9	−169.7	−334.6	−268.3
LLRI	0.317	0.395	0.329	0.314

Note: Refer to the discussion in Appendix 1 for details and interpretations of the various log-likelihood statistics. Significance at the 1% [5%] level is denoted by "**" ["*"] (one-tailed test).

Summary

These high-ability students seem quite rational in their college preferences: a college's perceived academic quality in the student's area of interest is of paramount importance. However, the students also give weight to perceptions of lifestyle, location, and quality of personal contact associated with a college. For colleges, these results suggest that academic and nonacademic lifestyle concerns are both of interest and concern to high-ability students. Colleges' student recruitment efforts should be directed in the first instance to the academic component of the college-going experience, but other aspects should definitely not be overlooked.

The general complexity of the college preference judgment formation process is noteworthy. All four composite perceptual ratings indices plus most of the college-specific effects are statistically significant. As with the college choice process, many factors are implicitly weighed by these high-ability students when they form preference judgments about colleges.

7. Antecedents of college choice behavior: Perception judgment formation

In this chapter, we seek to analyze the determinants of perceptions. The preference judgment formation process modeled in Chapter 6 indicated that four composite perceptual indices were important determinants of prior preference. We now wish to attempt to explain how objective college characteristics influence students' perceptions of colleges.

A major omitted variable problem arises in this perception formation judgment modeling effort. In our multistage college choice model, described in Chapter 2, we postulated that perceptions depend on both college characteristics and on the information environment. Since our focus in this study was on choice behavior, we made no effort to measure relevant aspects of the information environment possessed by each student.

The perception judgment formation modeling stage involves using composite ratings of perceptions and of colleges' attributes, both of which are needed to simplify the modeling task. The composite perception indices were developed in Chapter 6. The construction of composite college characteristics indices is described in the following section, prior to presenting and discussing the study's findings with regard to the determinants of perception judgment formation.

Construction of composite college characteristics indices

Prior to discussing the results of the perception formation modeling effort, it is necessary to describe some initial efforts at data reduction for the independent variables in the perception formation model. With regard to college characteristics, these efforts concerned constructing composite indices of academic quality, location, and nonacademic activities.

As described in Chapter 2, three major forces are presumed to influence a student's perception of a college: the actual objectively verifiable attributes which characterize a college, individual–institution interactions, and the information possessed by the student about the college. In this study, we did not measure the information environment associated with the college choice decision, since most of this information is presumably developed in the context of the search process.

Our primary source of objective variables to describe the colleges was the College Board's Annual Survey of Colleges (ASC). Among the individual–institution variables of interest are parental ties and distance (from the student's home to a college's campus). College-specific "brand name" effects may also be present. The complete list of independent variables included in our perception formation model is described in Table 7.1.

The objective college characteristics that are

Table 7.1. Definitions of the variables included in the perception judgment formation model

Group/variable	Definition
Academic character	
AQSCORE	Academic Quality Score (a composite index)
NUMMAJOR	Number of majors available
Institutional character	
MEN%	Percentage of all undergraduates who are male
COEDNESS	The degree of "coedness" at a campus. This is defined to be: 100-MEN% if MEN%>50; 50 if MEN%=50; MEN% if MEN%<50.
PRIVATE	An indicator variable which equals 1 if a college is private, and 0 otherwise.
UG%	Percentage of all students who are undergraduates.
Lifestyle aspects	
ACTSCORE	Activity Score (a composite index).
LOCSCORE	Location Score (a composite index).
Individual–institution interactions	
FATHER	An indicator variable that equals 1 if a student's father attended a college, and equals 0 otherwise.
MOTHER	An indicator variable that equals 1 if a student's mother attended a college, and equals 0 otherwise.
DISTANCE	The distance (in 000s of miles) from the campus of a college to the residence of a student.
College-specific effects	
COLLEGE1	An indicator variable that equals 1 for the most frequently mentioned college in terms of applications submitted by our 1,549 mail survey respondents, and equals 0 otherwise.
COLLEGE2 through COLLEGE7	Indicator variables for the second through seventh most frequently mentioned colleges in terms of applications submitted by our 1,549 mail survey respondents.

presumed to influence students' perceptions fall into three board categories: academic character, institutional character, and lifestyle aspects.

Academic character

With regard to academic character, a composite index was constructed to describe a college's academic quality, reputation, and prestige. This index includes a number of variables that measure student input quality, resource base, and other quality-related measures. The resulting academic quality composite index, AQSCORE, does not rely on a single measure of quality, but rather attempts to include a range of related indicators of academic quality. In addition, this index of eight different variables overcomes some missing-data problems that were present in the ASC data. The eight variables included in this index are defined and described in Table 7.2. A principal components factor analysis served to identify these variables. AQSCORE is the arithmetic mean of the available adjusted academic quality variables for a college, where the adjusted variables have been transformed to standard deviate form (mean of zero and standard deviation of one) so that their units are comparable. Missing values for a variable were ignored in this calculation.

In constructing the academic quality index, 27 colleges with 10 or more mentions in the mail survey had missing SAT data in the ASC data set. Supplementary data sources used to estimate the SAT scores of these colleges were taken from Fiske (1982), McClintock (1982), and *Barron's*

Profiles of American Colleges (1980). Where these secondary sources yielded multiple SAT scores, averages were used.

A second academic character variable is number of majors offered, NUMMAJOR. This variable captures both the breadth of the available academic offerings and the size of the educational institution.

Institutional character

Under the heading "institutional character," four variables are included: MEN%, the percentage of the students who are male; COEDNESS, a measure of how coeducational an institution is; PRIVATE, an indicator variable for whether a college is private; and UG%, the percentage of all students who are undergraduates. COEDNESS is an index that takes on the value 50 for a college where the male/female ratio is 1:1 and takes on

Table 7.2. *Variables used in the academic quality index*

Variable	Definition	Summary statistics		
		Mean	S.D.	n
SAT	Mean SAT scores of matriculants	527.6	60.6	372
SFRATIO	Student–faculty ratio	19.5	10.5	468
FACPHD%	Percentage of faculty with Ph.D. degrees	67.2	21.1	383
ADMIT%	Admission acceptance % (percentage of applicants who are admitted)	70.4	18.8	494
YIELD%	Yield rate % (percentage of admitted applicants who matriculate to a college)	51.8	16.2	487
FC1YR%	Percentage of freshmen who successfully complete their first year	86.5	9.0	512
FR2YR%	Percentage of freshmen who return for second year	79.9	11.3	473
GRAD%	Percentage of graduating students who go on for graduate studies	37.9	19.1	365

Note: These variables describe the 550 colleges to which students reported they applied one or more times in the mail survey responses. In forming the academic quality index, AQSCORE, these eight variables (in standard deviate form) were combined additively, except for the variables SFRATIO and ADMIT%, which were subtracted from the composite index. These subtractions occurred for these specific variables because they are of the "less is better" variety, while for all other variables "more is better."

values approaching zero as that ratio departs from 1:1 in either direction.

Lifestyle aspects

Two specific lifestyle aspects are included: the range of nonacademic activities offered, ACTSCORE, and a variable measuring location, LOCSCORE.

ACTSCORE is the sum of the number of the following activities available at a college: sports, performing arts, clubs, special programs and services for students, and special remedial programs. Thus, this variable is designed to capture a range of nonacademic activities supported by a college and to which a student would have access should he or she choose to attend.

LOCSCORE is a composite index constructed from three separate location variables available in the ASC data file. These three variables refer to the population of the nearest city/town and two other campus environment measures related to urbanness. These three raw variables were transformed to standard-deviate form and then averaged to develop the LOCSCORE composite index of location. Higher (lower) values of LOCSCORE denote more urban (rural) campus locations.

Individual–institution interactions

Parental ties to a college and distance are included in the perception-regression models to capture the potential influence of these relevant individual–institution interactions. Parental ties to a college may positively impact perceptions, partially due to the increased access to information about the college offered by this personal connection and partially due to students' values and views being influenced by their parents. Distance may be negatively related to perceptions, due to the difficulty associated with learning about distant colleges. Such difficulty may increase a student's uncertainty about a college, resulting in less favorable views being reported.

College-specific effects

College specific indicator variables for the seven colleges with 150 or more mentions by students in the mail survey were also included in the perception formation models. These variables measure the influence of the college's "brand name" above and beyond that which is reflected in the perceptual rating scores.

Functional form of the perceptual formation model

Since the perceptual ratings have been standardized to reflect relative perceptions, the independent variables must also be expressed in relative terms. The actual form of the perceptual formation models estimated was as follows:

$$R'_{scd} - R'_{sc*d} = \mathbf{b} \, (\mathbf{Z}_c - \mathbf{Z}_{c*})$$

where

s a student
c a college (and c^* represents a college other than college c)
R'_{scd} a standardized composite perceptual score for perceptual dimension d of college c for student s
$\mathbf{Z}_c$ the vector of independent variables in the perceptual formation model for college c.

In this equation, $\mathbf{b}$ is a vector of parameters (relative importance weights) to be estimated.

In estimating the model in the equation, one college alternative is "lost" for each student by the relativeness transformation. Only the unique number of college comparisons matters, not the number of colleges. Thus, a student with three colleges rated yields two unique comparisons (college 1 versus college 2, and college 1 versus college 3). Similarly, a student who rated two colleges provides just a single unique comparison (college 1 versus college 2).

Note also that the model does not contain a

constant term, since the variables and the model are all expressed in relative terms.

Results of estimating the perception formation model

Separate regression models were estimated for each of the four composite perceptual measures. All the independent variables described in Table 7.1 were included in each of these perceptual-regression models. Table 7.3 contains a summary of the results of these regression estimates. Detailed results may be found in Tables 7.4 to 7.7.

As may be noted, the goodness-of-fit of these models range from an R^2 of 0.076 for the LOCATION perception equation to an R^2 of 0.298 for the PERSONALNESS equation. These relatively low levels of goodness-of-fit are, however, not un-

Table 7.3. Summary results of estimating the perception formation model

Independent variables	Composite indices of the perceptual ratings (dependent variables)			
	ACADQUALITY	PERSONALNESS	LIFESTYLE	LOCATION
AQSCORE	+ + [1]		+ + [1]	
NUMMAJOR		− − [3]	+ + [2]	− −
MEN%	+ +	−	−	− − [4]
COEDNESS	− −		+	+ + [2]
PRIVATE		+ + [1]		
UG%	− − [2]	+ +	+ + [4]	
ACTSCORE		− −	+ + [3]	
LOCSCORE		− − [4]		
FATHER				
MOTHER				
DISTANCE		+ +		− − [3]
COLLEGE1	+ + [3]	− − [2]		+
COLLEGE2	+ + [5]			
COLLEGE3			+ + [5]	− − [1]
COLLEGE4		− −	+	+ + [5]
COLLEGE5				+
COLLEGE6	+ +		+	+ +
COLLEGE7	+ + [4]	− − [5]		
R^2	0.264	0.298	0.129	0.076
Number of observations	2,021	2,016	2,021	2,021

The coding in this table is as follows (all are one-tailed tests of significance):
"+ +" = a coefficient is significantly positive at the 0.01 level
"+" = a coefficient is significantly positive at the 0.05 level
"−" = a coefficient is significantly negative at the 0.05 level
"− −" = a coefficient is significantly negative at the 0.01 level.
The five most important variables in each regression equation, as measured by the standardized regression coefficients, are indicated by [1], [2], [3], [4], and [5]. Detailed regression results are reported in Tables 7.4 to 7.7.

Table 7.4. Results of estimating the perception formation model: *ACADQUALITY*[1]

Variable[2]	Coefficient estimate	Standard error	T-Ratio
AQSCORE	0.1792	0.0168	10.658
NUMMAJOR	−0.0015	0.0047	−0.319
MEN%	0.0035	0.0009	3.845
COEDNESS	−0.0041	0.0011	−3.688
PRIVATE	0.0403	0.0299	1.346
UG%	−0.0075	0.0009	−8.411
ACTSCORE	0.0018	0.0017	1.042
LOCSCORE	0.0267	0.0139	1.917
FATHER	0.0099	0.0396	0.251
MOTHER	0.0967	0.0530	1.825
DISTANCE	0.0123	0.0158	0.777
COLLEGE1	0.3143	0.0545	5.767
COLLEGE2	0.2161	0.0443	4.882
COLLEGE3	0.0521	0.5281	0.987
COLLEGE4	−0.0829	0.0504	−1.645
COLLEGE5	0.0966	0.0518	1.864
COLLEGE6	0.1482	0.0540	2.743
COLLEGE7	0.2927	0.0599	4.885

Summary statistics
$R^2 = 0.264$
Number of observations = 2,021

1. A linear-in-parameters functional form with additive disturbance terms was assumed. Estimation was via Ordinary Least Squares.
2. See Table 7.2 for definitions of these variables.

Table 7.5. Results of estimating the perception formation model: *PERSONALNESS*[1]

Variable[2]	Coefficient estimate	Standard error	T-Ratio
AQSCORE	−0.0293	0.0244	−1.203
NUMMAJOR	−0.0439	0.0068	−6.494
MEN%	−0.0029	0.0013	−2.202
COEDNESS	−0.0006	0.0016	−0.389
PRIVATE	0.5887	0.0434	13.567
UG%	0.0045	0.0013	3.438
ACTSCORE	−0.0064	0.0025	−2.603
LOCSCORE	−0.1105	0.0202	−5.464
FATHER	0.0970	0.0574	1.690
MOTHER	−0.1015	0.0769	−1.320
DISTANCE	0.0999	0.0229	4.355
COLLEGE1	−0.7396	0.0790	−9.361
COLLEGE2	0.0056	0.0642	0.088
COLLEGE3	0.0390	0.0766	0.509
COLLEGE4	−0.3041	0.0731	−4.161
COLLEGE5	−0.0911	0.0751	−1.212
COLLEGE6	0.0041	0.0783	0.052
COLLEGE7	−0.3943	0.0869	−4.539

Summary statistics
$R^2 = 0.298$
Number of observations = 2,016

1. A linear-in-parameters functional form with additive disturbance terms was assumed. Estimation was via Ordinary Least Squares.
2. See Table 7.2 for definitions of these variables.

expected. Recall that a key component of perceptions—the information environment—is not included in our regression equations. This omission reduces our ability to explain more of the variance in the composite perception rating indices. Also, our objectively verifiable variables are strictly quantitative in nature. They do not measure intangible quality dimensions well, if at all. For example, our measure of extracurricular activities, ACTSCORE, is a simple count of the available extracurricular activities. Quality considerations associated with such activities are unmeasured.

Academic quality perception formation

The results in Tables 7.3 and 7.4 indicate that our high-ability students' perceptions of college academic quality are primarily related to the following college characteristics:
• A college's actual academic quality (the higher, the better);

Table 7.6. Results of estimating the perception formation model: LIFESTYLE[1]

Variable[2]	Coefficient estimate	Standard error	T-Ratio
AQSCORE	0.0932	0.0198	4.710
NUMMAJOR	0.0253	0.0055	4.621
MEN%	−0.0035	0.0011	−3.252
COEDNESS	0.0029	0.0013	2.202
PRIVATE	−0.0088	0.0352	−0.249
UG%	0.0041	0.0011	3.844
ACTSCORE	0.0080	0.0020	3.996
LOCSCORE	0.0307	0.0164	1.869
FATHER	0.0712	0.0466	1.529
MOTHER	0.0083	0.0624	0.133
DISTANCE	0.0282	0.1862	1.516
COLLEGE1	0.0141	0.0641	0.221
COLLEGE2	−0.0117	0.0521	−0.225
COLLEGE3	0.2210	0.0621	3.556
COLLEGE4	0.1168	0.0593	1.969
COLLEGE5	−0.0796	0.0610	−1.305
COLLEGE6	0.1490	0.0636	2.344
COLLEGE7	0.0949	0.0705	1.347

Summary statistics
$R^2 = 0.129$
Number of observations = 2,021

1. A linear-in-parameters functional form with additive disturbance terms was assumed. Estimation was via Ordinary Least Squares.
2. See Table 7.2 for definitions of these variables.

Table 7.7 Results of estimating the perception formation model: LOCATION[1]

Variable[2]	Coefficient estimate	Standard error	T-Ratio
AQSCORE	0.0097	0.0277	0.352
NUMMAJOR	−0.0282	0.0077	−3.678
MEN%	−0.0056	0.0015	−3.793
COEDNESS	0.0070	0.0018	3.817
PRIVATE	−0.0304	0.0492	−0.618
UG%	−0.0009	0.0015	−0.592
ACTSCORE	0.0003	0.0028	0.110
LOCSCORE	0.0114	0.0230	0.495
FATHER	0.0811	0.0651	1.245
MOTHER	0.0740	0.0872	0.849
DISTANCE	−0.0990	0.0260	−3.804
COLLEGE1	0.2042	0.0897	2.277
COLLEGE2	0.0293	0.0728	0.403
COLLEGE3	−0.5239	0.0869	−6.029
COLLEGE4	0.3108	0.0829	3.747
COLLEGE5	0.2103	0.0853	2.466
COLLEGE6	−0.2312	0.0889	−2.601
COLLEGE7	−0.0458	0.0986	−0.464

Summary statistics
$R^2 = 0.076$
Number of observations = 2,021

1. A linear-in-parameters functional form with additive disturbance terms was assumed. Estimation was via Ordinary Least Squares.
2. See Table 7.2 for definitions of these variables.

• A college's undergraduate concentration (the smaller the undergraduate student composition in the total student body, the better; the greater the graduate student composition, the better); and

• A college's gender mix (the greater the concentration of men, the better).

In addition, there are some college-specific effects in operation here.

Actual academic quality, as proxied by our composite index AQSCORE, is the primary determinant of perceived academic quality. In addition, colleges with well-recognized academic quality also tend to have substantial numbers of graduate students in their student bodies. Thus, the role of UG% is not unexpected.

It is also significant that ACTSCORE and LOCSCORE are not determinants of academic quality perception. ACTSCORE and LOCSCORE have no particular theoretical relationship to academic quality, so their irrelevance is of note in judging the performance of this regression model. Our empirical results are consistent with this *a priori* theory.

Personalness perception formation

The results in Tables 7.3 and 7.5 indicate that our high-ability students' perceptions of college "personalness" are primarily related to the following characteristics:

- Whether a college is private ("privateness" is positively perceived);
- A college's breadth of course offerings, as proxied by number of majors (the more majors—a correlate of college size—the less perceived "personalness");
- A college's location (more "ruralness" is viewed positively);
- Distance from a student's home to a college's campus (more distant colleges are viewed as being more "personal"); and
- A college's undergraduate concentration (the more the college's student body is concentrated in undergraduate students, the better).

There are also some college-specific effects in evidence.

Small, private colleges are perceived to be especially personal. Recall that the number of majors (NUMMAJOR) and breadth of extracurricular activities (ACTSCORE) are correlates of college size. Thus, larger public colleges are, in general, viewed as being less "personal." Such colleges tend to be in urban areas; small private colleges are often in rural areas. Thus, the negative LOCSCORE effect is consistent with these other results.

A priori theoretical considerations would suggest that college quality should have no influence on perceived "personalness." The evidence is consistent with such a view, since AQSCORE is not significantly related to PERSONALNESS.

Lifestyle perception formation

The results in Tables 7.3 and 7.6 indicate that our high-ability students' perceptions of college lifestyle are primarily related to the following characteristics:

- A college's academic quality (the higher the better);
- The size of a college, as proxied by number of majors and breadth of available extracurricular activities (the more the better);
- The college's undergraduate concentration (the higher the better);
- Degree of "coedness" (a balanced enrollment split between men and women being preferred).

Several college-specific effects are in evidence.

The results are in accord with *a priori* expectations. Larger colleges are, in general, preferred. This is sensible since larger schools offer more and varied living, nonacademic, athletic, and extracurricular opportunities. However, AQSCORE is the primary determinant of perceived lifestyle. Thus, colleges with high quality—and the associated concentration on academic aspects of the educational experience—also are viewed as being desirable from a lifestyle perception viewpoint. These findings suggest that both academic and nonacademic considerations are reflected in our students' perceptions of lifestyle.

Location perception formation

Our model for LOCATION has relatively poor statistical performance, compared to the other three composite indices. Thus, these findings should be taken as tentative.

The results in Table 7.3 and 7.7 indicate that our high-ability students' perceptions of college location are primarily related to the following characteristics:

- College gender mix (single-sex institutions are viewed negatively);
- Distance (colleges farther away from a student's residence are viewed negatively);
- College size, as proxied by numbers of majors (larger colleges are viewed less favorably).

Strong college-specific effects are in evidence:

Five of the seven college-specific effects are statistically significant.

An ideal location for a college is close to a student's home, in a nonurban setting (since larger colleges tend to be located in urban centers), and with a nicely balanced coed student population.

Conclusions

Even with a relatively low level of statistical fit, our perception judgment formation equations demonstrate interpretable and significant linkages between objectively verifiable college characteristics and perception ratings indices. The results are, in general, quite consistent with *a priori* expectations. Research more centrally focused than this study on the determinants of students' college perceptions could examine a larger array of college attributes, students' levels of information about colleges, and possible individual differences among students in the factors influencing perception judgment formation. The more limited analysis reported here suggests that such research efforts would meet with reasonable success in demonstrating interpretable linkages between college characteristics and student perceptions.

It is interesting that many factors (statistically significant variables) appear to be at work in influencing the formation of college perception judgments for our high-ability students. As with our findings about the determinants of college choice behavior and preference judgment formation, many considerations are at work with regard to the determinants of perceptions.

8. Other factors influencing college choice behavior: Campus visits and post-admissions contacts

In this chapter, we focus on two other factors which may influence college choice behavior: campus visits and post-admissions contacts. Here, we study the role, incidence, and influence that such visits and contacts exert on college choice behavior.

Our interest in post-admissions contacts is based on several considerations. First, such contacts are between a college and its admitted applicants. Thus, they involve genuinely interested students which the college has already identified as being academically acceptable. Second, these contacts may be managed and influenced to some extent by colleges if it's worthwhile to invest resources, time, and effort in so doing.

For campus visits, we may assume that students visit only colleges in which they have considerable interest. Thus, the act of visiting is an important signal to the college of the student's interest. If the act of visiting a college's campus is a good signal as to a student's ultimate enrollment choices, then once again colleges might wish to attempt to manage this process with care.

Direct mail appears to have assumed the role as the primary student recruitment marketing tool in college admissions. However, direct mail is efficient (inexpensive) but not effective on a per-student-contacted basis. Other things (high school visits, participation in college fairs/nights, campus visits, and post-admissions contacts) are more personal and are likely to be more effective but not as efficient (more costly) on a per-student-contacted basis. The key issue concerns the relative degrees of effectiveness and efficiency of alternative recruiting tools. In studying various forms of post-admissions contacts, we wish to address the effectiveness issue directly.

Some methodological issues

Our study is of the cross-sectional variety. It is not experimental in nature. This raises some important issues with regard to assessing the role and influence of campus visits and post-admissions contacts on college choice behavior. The crux of the issue concerns causality assessment and direction of causality.

If we observe a high correlation between campus visits or post-admissions contacts and choice behavior, we still may not be able to classify such a factor as being causally related to behavior. The problem is that we did not know the student's degree of interest prior to the visit or contact.

In our surveying, we asked students to identify the nature of any post-admissions contacts with the colleges to which they were admitted and also to identify the colleges (if any) that they had visited. We did not ask them who initiated the contact, nor did we ask when the campus visit occurred.

Thus, the causality-assessment problem relates to the following types of issues: Did a student initiate a contact because he or she was particularly interested in a college, or did the contact increase the student's prior interest? Did a student visit a campus because he or she was already highly interested in the college, or did the campus visit spark the student's high interest? Probably both kinds of influence occur, but it would be a serious mistake to assume that the direction of causality flows only from the contact to the interest.

In conclusion, then, our empirical results should be taken only as suggestive of patterns, and not as definitive findings. Still, they represent a large-scale effort to examine this aspect of college choice behavior.

Empirical results: Four key numbers

Four key numbers should be noted as we turn our attention to the empirical results:

Number of students who replied to the telephone survey	= 1,183
Number of admissions offers	= 3,988
Mean number of colleges to which these students were admitted	= 3.4
Probability of choosing any college (given that it was in a student's choice set and that the student was admitted to the college)	= 29.4%

Each of the 3,988 offers to the 1,183 students had, on average, a 29.4 percent chance of being selected (1183/3988 expressed in percentage terms). These numbers represent base-line re-

sults with which other figures and results will be compared.

Empirical results: Campus visits

To learn about various college options, students may consult a variety of sources. An actual visit to the campus of a college is a particularly notable source of information. It provides an opportunity for a student (and his parents) to view the living environment and meet with a number of relevant people (faculty, other college officials, and other students).

A feature of our campus visit data should be noted. These data do not include information on when the visit actually occurred. Thus, a campus visit might have occurred during the early search phase of the college selection process or it might have been a true post-admissions contact, occurring after the student had been notified of being admitted.

Our high-ability students engaged in a substantial amount of college campus visit activity: 91.7 percent (1,085 of 1,183) of our respondents made at least one campus visit and 64.5 percent of all 3,988 admissions involved such a visit. Our survey respondents reported that their opinions of colleges generally improved as a result of campus visits. Indeed, 52.6 percent of campus visits led to a student reporting a more positive view of the college, while in only 9.9 percent of the visits did the student report that the experience ultimately resulted in a more negative view of the college. Our respondents reported no change in their views of colleges for 37.5 percent of the visits.

Table 8.1 contains some information on visiting patterns and actual choices. Knowing nothing about a student's campus visit activities or college preferences, an average choice set size of 3.4 colleges implies that each college has, on average, about a 29.4 percent chance of being chosen. However, as the data in Table 8.1 indi-

Table 8.1. Correlation of campus visits and college choices

	Frequency of choosing a college (%)	
	Given a campus visit	Given no campus visit
All students	39.7	12.6
Students making 1 visit only	82.5	19.2
Students making at least 1 visit	43.3	9.9
Students making at least 2 visits	28.9	6.5

Note: Base for "all students"   = 1,183 students
        Base for "1 visit only"   =   291 students
        Base for "at least 1 visit" = 1,085 students
        Base for "at least 2 visits" =   794 students.

cate, knowing something about campus visit activities can considerably change these base-line figures. Across all students and campus visit frequencies, if we know that a student has visited a campus, then we can revise our 29.4 percent choice-probability figure to 39.7 percent for such a visited college. Furthermore, 82.5 percent of students visiting only one campus ultimately enroll at that college.

Our data support the conclusion that students who visit a college tend to choose the visited college. The strength of our findings almost suggests that there may be an empirical "law of campus visits": "Students who visit tend to choose the visited college." This is no doubt because a visit is a sign that a student has a high degree of interest in a college.

There are a variety of implications to colleges that flow from this finding. First, colleges should find it worthwhile to devote considerable attention to managing the campus visit process. A campus visit is not a minor matter in the minds and behavior of students. Second, they should try to encourage applicants, prospective applicants, and admitted applicants to visit their campuses. Third, colleges should attempt to make it easy (and as low-cost as possible) for students to make campus visits. Note that here, "cost" is used in the senses of monetary, time, and "red tape" considerations.

Empirical results: Post-admissions contacts

By definition, post-admissions contacts occur after admissions decisions are communicated to students, but before students actually choose a college. Such contacts are especially interesting because they take place so close to the actual point at which the college choice decision occurs.

The data in Tables 8.2, 8.3, and 8.4 suggest that post-admissions contacts are infrequent, but apparently almost always positive. Only 52.2 percent of all admissions involved some such contact (with one or more contacts with one or more colleges). The corresponding figures for contact by mail, telephone, and meeting are 37.4, 21.9, and 19.4 percent, respectively.

The incidence of post-admissions contacts by

Table 8.2. Frequency of post-admissions contacts[1]

No. of contacts	Contact by any means (overall)	Contact by letter	Contact by telephone	Contact by meeting
0	47.8%	62.6%	78.1%	80.6%
1	23.0	24.5	19.1	11.3
2	14.6	9.4	2.5	5.8
3	7.0	2.5	.3	1.6
4	3.8	.6	.0	.6
5+	3.8	.4	.0	.2
	100.0%	100.0%	100.0%	100.0%[2]

1. These data reflect the responses of 1,183 students.
2. Due to rounding, some totals do not add to 100.0%.

Table 8.3. Incidence of various types of post-admissions contacts

Contact with	Contact incidence (%)		
	Letter	Telephone	Meeting
Dean/President	3.6	.3	1.3
Faculty member	15.8	3.4	9.5
Coach	3.5	2.1	1.1
Other students	4.1	4.8	4.4
Alumni	9.0	8.8	5.3
Admissions personnel	12.6	4.0	6.4
Honors program	2.4	.5	1.4
Other	4.2	1.2	1.6

Note: These data reflect the responses of 1,183 students.

various means (letter, telephone, and meeting) by different types of people affiliated with a college are displayed in Table 8.3. Contact by letter is most often by a faculty member (about 15.8 percent of all students reported one or more contacts by letter from a faculty member), with admissions personnel running a close second in frequency of contact. Alumni are most frequently associated with telephone post-admissions contacts. For personal meetings, the three most frequent post-admissions contacts are with faculty members, admissions personnel, and alumni.

The results in Table 8.4 suggest that the more personal the contact, the greater the chance that it will have a positive impact on the student. Contact by letter results in particularly positive influences on the students in 26.7–40.2 percent of the contact occasions, across the various types of contact people. The corresponding results for telephone and meeting contacts are 30.4–50.0 percent and 47.3–66.0 percent, respectively. Stated another way, the typical post-admissions contact by letter results in no particular influence on the student; however, the typical contact in person during a meeting results in a positive impression being left with the student.

The data in Table 8.4 also suggest that sharp differences among the "contact" persons do not seem to exist. For example, for contact by letter, the most positive reported contact was with honors programs, where 40.2 percent of these contacts were reported as positive; and the least positive reported contact was with alumni, where

Table 8.4. Reported influence of various types of post-admissions contacts

Contact with	Reported effect of a contact (%), given that a contact occurred					
	Letter		Telephone		Meeting	
	Positive	Negative	Positive	Negative	Positive	Negative
Dean/President	34.5	.0	50.0	.0	66.0	4.0
Faculty member	29.4	.6	44.5	1.5	59.7	4.2
Coach	28.9	.7	42.2	1.2	59.5	2.4
Other students	34.0	2.4	37.3	.5	57.1	6.2
Alumni	26.7	.6	31.9	.9	58.7	4.2
Admissions personnel	28.1	.8	42.8	1.9	53.1	5.9
Honors program	40.2	1.0	50.0	5.0	47.3	9.1
Other	28.0	2.4	30.4	6.5	51.6	9.7

Note: These data reflect the responses of 1,183 students. The neutral responses are not shown, since: positive + neutral + negative = 100.0%.

26.7 percent of these contacts were reported as positive. The "positives" for honors programs versus alumni letter contacts is only in the ratio of 1.5:1. Thus, there is not really that much difference across the various types of contacts. It appears that, for post-admissions contacts, "a contact is a contact is a contact."

Given these findings, it is puzzling that post-admissions contacts occur so infrequently. Of course, cost–benefit considerations are relevant here, as are logistical considerations. The time between admissions decision and reply date may be too tight for large-scale post-admissions contact efforts. *But,* what about selective contact efforts directed toward specific students or types of students? The thoughtful management of post-admissions contacts appears to be a worthwhile endeavor for a college.

Concluding remarks

The true effect of campus visits and post-admissions contacts on choice is uncertain. For campus visits, we don't know the student's pre- and post-visit levels of interest; for post-admissions contacts, we don't know who initiated the contact. Still, these results are suggestive of some important patterns. Further research, with pre- and post-measures of a student's interest in a college before and after the contact, is needed to clarify the role and influence of campus visits and post-admissions contacts on college choice.

9. Changes in college choice after the initial decision

College admissions officers have, in recent years, reported increasing numbers of "no-shows"— students who simultaneously accept admissions offers and submit deposits to hold places at multiple colleges, deferring decisions concerning the colleges in which they will actually enroll. Because of this phenomenon, the college choices reported to us by students in the telephone follow-up interviews might potentially differ from final enrollment choices for a sizable number of students. Apart from students changing their college choices, others might decide not to attend any college in the fall. If changes in college plans occurring over the summer months before entry to college were influenced, in particular, by monetary considerations, these monetary influences on student choices would not be reflected in the main study results.

For these reasons, students in the study sample were contacted again in the fall of 1984 to obtain information concerning the colleges in which they had actually enrolled. This enrollment information was then compared with students' earlier reports concerning college choices. The main findings of this follow-up survey are summarized below.

Data collection procedure

In November 1984, respondents to the earlier survey stages were asked to indicate: (1) whether they attended college in the fall of 1984 (and, if they did not attend, the main reasons for not attending); (2) if enrolled in college in the fall of 1984, the name of the college in which the student was enrolled and whether this was the same college he or she had planned to attend as of the end of high school (i.e., in May/June 1984); if it was not the same college, the main reason for the change was requested.

Questionnaires were accompanied by a cover letter from the president of the College Board thanking students for taking part in the main study. A brief summary of main findings was also enclosed as a tangible expression of appreciation and as a means of motivating response to the follow-up.

Since our records contained students' home addresses but not college addresses, questionnaires were sent to students' homes. The mailing was timed to arrive just before Thanksgiving, since it was assumed that a substantial number of those students residing at college would visit home during Thanksgiving and would thus receive the questionnaire directly. For students not at home during this period, the mailing would have to be forwarded to the students' campus addresses.

The sample for the follow-up study included all students for whom college choice information had been obtained in the main study. This sample included: (1) students who applied to only one college and who were not included in the telephone survey (n = 325) and (2) students who applied to more than one college and with whom telephone interviews were completed in May/June (n = 1,183). Thus, the total number of cases included in the follow-up survey was 1,508.

Findings

Response rates

A total of 909 completed questionnaires were received from the 1,508 students in the follow-up sample. This represents an overall response rate of 60.3 percent. This relatively high response rate is generally consistent with the high rates experienced in the earlier study phases and is about as high as could be expected for a mail survey of this kind with no follow-up to nonrespondents. This experience indicates that it is possible to obtain a reaonably high response to a survey of college freshmen conducted by means of a brief questionnaire mailed to their home addresses in the fall.

Analyses of nonrespondents and respondents by sex, class rank, parental income, and SAT scores are provided in Table 9.1. Only negligible differences exist between respondents and nonrespondents on each of these variables, and these analyses show no evidence of response bias. It is worth noting as well that the original study sample of 2,000 was selected so that equal numbers of cases would fall in each of five intervals for average SAT scores, and the follow-up respondents are also distributed approximately evenly over these intervals.

Although Table 9.1 shows no evidence of nonresponse bias, it is possible that the variable of interest in the follow-up study—changes in col-

Table 9.1. Comparison of fall follow-up respondents and nonrespondents on selected background variables

	Nonrespondents	Respondents
Average SAT score		
550–599	19.1%	19.1%
600–649	20.8	18.2
650–699	19.3	19.6
700–749	21.7	20.6
750–800	19.1	22.5
	100.0%	100.0%
High school class rank		
2nd tenth	18.9%	17.4%
Top tenth	81.1	82.6
	100.0%	100.0%
Gender		
Male	63.8%	61.2%
Female	36.2	38.8
	100.0%	100.0%
Self-reported parental gross income		
$30,000 or less	24.2%	25.6%
$30,001–$49,999	36.6	37.4
$50,000 or more	39.2	37.0
	100.0%	100.0%

lege plans—has a relationship to response, but not to these background variables. If students who changed college plans were either more or less likely to return our questionnaire, our estimates of incidence of such changes could be biased.

College nonattendance

Only 7 of the 909 respondents stated that they did not enroll in college in the fall of 1984. Of these seven, only two indicated that monetary factors (lack of money or need to take a job) were the main reasons for changes in college plans.

Four of the seven provided general/personal reasons (e.g., "felt I needed to take some time off").

These findings need to be related to the time frame of our study. An additional seven students were not included in the fall follow-up survey because they stated during telephone interviews in May or June that they had decided not to attend college immediately after high school. Most of these students had decided by that time to take advantage of other educational opportunities (e.g., study abroad under a student exchange program, or participation in a field study for a scientific project).

Changes in college choice

Information collected in our follow-up study permits changes in college choice to be examined in two ways.

First, since respondents attending college in the fall provided the name of the colleges in which they had actually enrolled, the college listed on the follow-up questionnaire could be compared with the college choice reported by the students earlier. For students who applied to only one college, the single colleges applied to were taken to be the earlier choices. For other students, earlier college choices were determined in telephone interviews conducted in May and June.

Second, students also indicated on the follow-up questionnaire whether the college enrolled in was "the same college you were planning to attend, as of the end of your senior year in high school."

There were 902 respondents to this part of the follow-up questionnaire: the original 909 less the 7 students not attending any college. Of these 902, only 9 listed different colleges in the November follow-up survey from the ones they had indicated earlier. Only one of these students with discrepant choices was from the group initially reporting application to only one college, substantiating the assumption that virtually all the students listing only one application on the March questionnaire would ultimately attend the colleges listed. The other eight students with discrepant choices listed different colleges from the ones indicated as the colleges chosen at the time of the telephone interview.

A slightly larger number (24 students) reported that they had changed their choice of college to attend after the end of the senior year in high school. Of these 24 students, 5 were students who also listed different colleges in the spring and fall. However, 19 of these 24 students listed the same colleges on the follow-up questionnaire as the ones named as their choices in an earlier phase of the study. The reasons given by these students for changing colleges, which are reported in Table 9.2, shed some light on this apparent contradiction.

Seven students who listed the same colleges in the spring and fall indicated they were not accepted to a preferred school from a wait list. Although they may perceive themselves as having changed their college choice (since they would have attended a different college had they been accepted from the wait list), the choice reported to us in May or June is properly consistent with the one listed in the fall. The 12 additional students reporting changes in college choices, but listing the same colleges in the spring and fall,

Table 9.2. Reasons given for changes in college choice

Reason	College listed in follow-up was	
	same as in earlier report	different from earlier report
Money-related reason	12	3
Family moved	0	1
Not accepted from wait list	7	0
Accepted from wait list	0	1
	19	5

all gave reasons relating to college costs or financial aid. We assume that these students attend colleges that were not their most preferred colleges, but that the decisions to do so were made prior to the telephone interviews. Some of these students may not have taken literally our question concerning consistency of college attended with the "college you were planning to attend, as of the end of your senior year in high school."

Discussion

Several general conclusions are supported by the findings of the follow-up study discussed in this chapter. With respect to college attendance, a very small percentage (roughly 1 percent) of students like those in our respondent group (SAT-taking high-ability students who filed college applications in their senior year of high school) fail to attend college in the fall immediately after high school. Since nonrespondents to our initial spring questionnaire on college applications may have included an additional number of students not applying to college, this result may underestimate the percentage of students from the population we sampled who do not go directly to college from high school.

Those not attending college are made up primarily of students deferring college study either to pursue other educational opportunities or to take time off for personal reasons.

While almost no students in our sample reported not enrolling in any college due to lack of money, this finding needs to be interpreted in context. Our sample did not include students who had not applied to colleges or who had not taken the SAT because they had already ruled out going to college, whether because college going was perceived to be too costly or for other reasons.

With respect to changes in college plans following high school graduation, students reporting in March application to and acceptance at only one college will almost certainly enroll in the college named. For students choosing among two or more

admissions offers, choices made by May to late June are very likely to be followed through. Only a tiny fraction of students enroll in different colleges from the ones named as final choices in telephone interviews in May and June.

The findings of this follow-up survey validate to a very large degree the college choice data analyzed in the main study. Overwhelmingly, students enrolled in the schools they had reported earlier as their choices. Neither monetary nor other reasons caused many students to change from college choices reported in May and June.

The findings of this follow-up survey appear to be at variance with reports of college admissions officers that significant numbers of students simultaneously submit deposits to hold multiple places in colleges and ultimately fail to enroll in one or more colleges whose admissions offers they have accepted—the "no-show" phenomenon. Since these reports are certainly accurate, we believe that our contrary finding of a low incidence of changes in college choice is most likely a function of the timing of and procedures for the telephone interviews. Students in our sample were called starting the second week of May. Only students stating they had made a choice of college to attend were interviewed, with other students called back at a later date. Callbacks for some students extended into mid-to-late June. Thus, our data are not inconsistent with the known fact that a sizable minority of students accepted to selective colleges defer decisions past the beginning of May. Experience in the interview portion of the study and in this follow-up suggests, however, that stable choices have been reached by nearly all students like those in our sample by the end of June. It appears that surveys during the May and June period can capture reports of college choices that are the same as fall enrollment decisions for about 98 percent of such students.

Appendix 1. An overview of the multinomial logit model

In this appendix, we provide a brief description of the multinomial logit model that is used extensively in this study. Also, some key statistical details and tests associated with using this model are described. For further details of the model as applied in the college choice context, the interested reader is referred to Kohn, Manski, and Mundel (1976), Chapman (1977, 1979), Punj and Staelin (1978), and Manski and Wise (1983). Technically oriented readers may wish to consult McFadden (1974), Gensch and Recker (1979), Hensher and Johnson (1981), Maddala (1983), and Ben-Akiva and Lerman (1985) for more extensive discussion of the multinomial logit model. A particularly complete, up-to-date, and applied treatment of discrete choice models is provided in Ben-Akiva and Lerman (1985).

The model

The multinomial logit model expresses the probability of choosing an alternative (e.g., a college) from a choice set (e.g., all colleges to which a student has been admitted) as depending on the relative value or utility of the alternative compared to other available alternatives. The multinomial logit model is a well-defined probability-of-choice model: each alternative will have a non-negative (zero or positive) chance of being chosen, and the sum of the probabilities across all alternatives in a choice set will be equal to 1.0. Specifically, the mathematical form of the multinomial logit model is as follows:

$$P_{ij} = \frac{\exp(V_{ij})}{\exp(V_{i1}) + \exp(V_{i2}) + \cdots + \exp(V_{i,J_i})} \tag{A1}$$

where

i	a decision-maker (a student)
j	an alternative (a college)
J_i	the total number of alternatives (colleges) in the choice set of decision-maker (student) i
P_{ij}	the probability that decision-maker (student) i chooses alternative (college) j
V_{ij}	the overall value or utility which decision-maker (student) i derives from alternative (college) j
$\exp(\cdot)$	the exponentiation function.

To operationalize this model, the form of the value or utility function, V, must be specified. A linear additive functional form is typically assumed, although it is important to note that (a) the model itself is of a nonlinear form, due to the presence of the exponentiation functions; (b) the variables themselves may be nonlinear compositions or interactions of other variables; and (c) linear additive functional forms are often parsimonious (simple) representations of more complicated functional relationships, especially within a limited relevant range of variation in a sample of data. Assuming that there are K relevant variables which the decision-makers (students) implicitly combine to form overall value or utility assessments of each alternative (college), V may be defined as follows:

$$V_{ij} = \theta_1 Z_{ij1} + \cdots + \theta_k Z_{ijk} + \cdots + \theta_K Z_{ijK} \tag{A2}$$

where

θ_k the relative importance of attribute k to the decision-makers (students) in forming their overall value judgments about the worth of an alternative (college)

Z_{ijk} the numerical value of attribute k associated with alternative (college) j to decision-maker (student) i.

The relative importance weights $\theta_1, \cdots, \theta_K$ are the parameters to be estimated. In the college choice context, the Z variables may include such factors as college characteristics (such as the size of a college or its tuition level), perceptual ratings of colleges (such as the perceived quality of a college by a student), and individual–institution interactions (such as the amount of scholarship aid awarded by a college to a student).

As a statistical model, the multinomial logit model possesses a number of desirable features. First, it represents a choice process in a natural fashion. Students are viewed as making a specific choice from among a given (and specific) set of colleges. Second, it is a natural probabilistic choice model. The probabilities derived satisfy the usual laws of probabilities (non-negativity and summing to 1.0). Third, the statistical properties of the parameter estimates are familiar. In particular, they are (asymptotically) normally distributed, so standard tests of statistical significance about the estimated relative importances can be made. Fourth, the probabilistic choice model allows strong statements to be made about the magnitude of the influence of the variables influencing choice. For example, the model will provide quantitative estimates of the trade-offs between

financial aid and choice probabilities. Thus, it is possible to derive an estimate of by how much choice probabilities (or, in the aggregate, market shares) will change with changes in financial aid offered to students.

Estimation of the multinomial logit model's parameters

Maximum-likelihood techniques are used to estimate the parameters of the multinomial logit model. This essentially involves a series of non-linear regressions, where the maximum-likelihood technique attempts to choose values of $\boldsymbol{\theta}$ such that the statistical fit between the observed choices and the predicted choices is maximized.

In our study, students reported on the rank order of their three most preferred colleges at the application stage (the unconstrained prior preference measures). At the choice stage, they were asked to indicate their chosen college, plus their second and third choices. By asking students to indicate their second and third preferences/choices, efficient estimation of the multinomial-logit-model parameters may be achieved by using the explosion techniques described in Chapman and Staelin (1982). This explosion procedure involves generating extra choice observations from the ranked preference/choice data for each respondent. Extra observations (choice sets) improve the statistical precision of the (multinomial logit) model's parameter estimates (relative importances). Exact statistical testing procedures exist to determine if such explosion procedures may be used. The key condition to be satisfied before invoking the explosion procedure is that the students' relative importances must be (statistically) identical for first-choice and for subsequent lower-choice decisions.

Statistical goodness-of-fit analysis

The most frequently used statistical goodness-of-fit measure for multinomial logit models is the

Table A1.1. Reported log-likelihood ratio index statistics in previous college choice studies

	Reported log-likelihood ratio index statistic	Sample size	Number of variables in choice model
Kohn, Manski, and Mundel (1976)			
Illinois students			
Low income	0.382	997	15
Medium income	0.286	990	15
High income	0.269	1028	15
North Carolina students			
Low income	0.272	1623	15
Medium income	0.302	749	15
High income	0.319	760	15
Chapman (1977, 1979)			
High-income students			
Engineering and science	0.128	1152	10
Liberal arts	0.097	532	10
Fine arts	0.146	513	10
Medium- and low-income students			
Engineering and science	0.158	1012	12
Liberal arts	0.162	183	12
Fine arts	0.160	278	12

Note: "Sample size" refers to the number of choice sets available for analysis.

log-likelihood ratio index (LLRI), which is defined as:

$$LLRI = 1 - \frac{LL(\theta = \theta^*)}{LL(\theta = 0)} \qquad (A3)$$

where $LL(\theta = \theta^*)$ is the value of the log-likelihood function at the maximum-likelihood estimate θ^* (sometimes called the *final log-likelihood* [final LL] value) and $LL(\theta = 0)$ is the value of the log-likelihood function evaluated at the point $\theta = 0$ (sometimes called the *initial log-likelihood* [Initial LL] value). LLRI is bounded by 0 and 1; thus it has an analogous interpretation to R^2 in standard regression analysis.

Reported values of LLRI from some previous college choice studies which used the multino-

mial logit model are displayed in Table A1.1. The range of values is about 0.09 to 0.38. The base of comparison in calculating the LLRI is the equiprobable choice model—a model in which every alternative has an equal chance of being chosen. Given the nature of the college choice process—with extensive search for satisfactory college alternatives—this is quite a strong base model. Thus, while modest improvements over this equiprobable model are undoubtedly possible, it should not be expected that perfect models would ever be developed (i.e., models with LLRI values near 1.0). Indeed, the data reported in Table A1.1 substantiate this observation.

The LLRI value from the study by Manski and Wise (1983) is not reported in Table A1.1. Manski and Wise (1983, p. 111) included four noncollege alternatives in their college choice model: (1) labor force participation (the full-time working option); (2) military enlistment; (3) homemaking; and (4) a combination of part-time school and part-time work. Alternative-specific indicator variables (dummy variables) were used in their model to account for these noncollege options. These variables had substantial effects in their model (t-ratios of -5.3 to -14.6). The inclusion of these noncollege options makes their college choice model fundamentally different from those in Kohn, Manski, and Mundel (1976) and Chapman (1977, 1979). Thus, the LLRI value of 0.501 reported in Manski and Wise (1983) is not comparable to the other LLRI values from pure college choice studies.

Other goodness-of-fit measures are sometimes used to describe how well the multinomial logit model performs. The correlation of actual and predicted choices (aggregated across all choice sets) provides another useful measure of performance of the model. Punj and Staelin (1978) report the results of an external predictive-validity assessment, where they used a multinomial logit model to predict the choices of the following year's students. Their predictions were excellent approximations of actual enrollment patterns.

Hypothesis testing and pooling tests

Standard types of hypothesis tests may be used to test the statistical significance of individual parameter estimates in the multinomial logit model. For example, the traditional t-ratio (the ratio of a coefficient estimate to its standard error) may be employed to test whether an individual coefficient is different from zero.

We conduct a number of pooling tests in this study. To test the hypothesis that N groups of choice data are characterized by the same underlying parameter vector (including the same variables), a standard pooling-test procedure is followed. The model is estimated separately for each of the N groups and then a single pooled model is also estimated. The relevant test statistic is:

$$-2 \{LL (\theta_P^*) - [LL (\theta_1^*) + \cdots + LL (\theta_n^*) + \cdots + LL (\theta_N^*)]\}$$

where $LL(\theta_P^*)$ is the maximum log-likelihood function value for the pooled data and $LL (\theta_n^*)$ is the maximum log-likelihood function value for subgroup n. This test statistic is asymptotically distributed chi-squared with $K(N-1)$ degrees of freedom, where K is the number of parameters estimated in each model (Wald 1943; Watson and Westin 1975; Ben-Akiva and Lerman 1985, pp. 194–204). To use this pooling test in this precise form, each of the subgroups of choice sets must be characterized by the same variables as the pooled data. Other issues associated with such pooling testing are discussed in Ben-Akiva and Lerman (1985, pp. 194–204). We use pooling tests such as this to examine the explosion possibilities inherent in rank-ordered choice sets (Chapman and Staelin 1982) and also to test for individual differences.

Appendix 2. The mail questionnaire

This appendix contains a copy of the questions used in the mail questionnaire that was employed in this study. The questions are in the exact order in which they were arranged on the actual questionnaire. A mailing label with the student's address was included at the top. The initial introductory instructions/sentences were as follows: "We need the information on the label below in order to relate your responses to this questionaire to other information you have previously provided to the College Board. If any of this information is incorrect, please give the correct information in the space to the right of the label."

Question 1: To which colleges have you applied? Please list these colleges below and provide the other information requested for each college.

Colleges applied to College	City/State	Application status at this time				Financial aid
		Haven't heard yet	*Accepted*	*Not accepted*	*On the wait list*	*Did you (or will you) apply for financial aid? [circle Yes or No]*
―――	―――	☐	☐	☐	☐	Yes No
―――	―――	☐	☐	☐	☐	Yes No
―――	―――	☐	☐	☐	☐	Yes No
―――	―――	☐	☐	☐	☐	Yes No
―――	―――	☐	☐	☐	☐	Yes No
―――	―――	☐	☐	☐	☐	Yes No
―――	―――	☐	☐	☐	☐	Yes No
―――	―――	☐	☐	☐	☐	Yes No
―――	―――	☐	☐	☐	☐	Yes No
―――	―――	☐	☐	☐	☐	Yes No

Note: If you have applied to any college under an early action or early decision plan, but a decision on your application has been deferred until a later notification date, please mark the column "Haven't Heard Yet."

Question 2: Assume that you will be accepted at all the colleges you listed and the cost to you and your family would be about the same at any of these colleges (and therefore not a factor in your choice).

Then, which of these colleges would be your:

First Choice: _____

Second Choice: _____

Third Choice: _____

Question 3: Please list other colleges that you did *not* apply to, but to which you gave serious consideration. For this question, "serious consideration" means that you did something more than just thinking about applying. For example, include colleges in this group if you sent away for information from the college or for application materials, or if you were interviewed by a representative or alumnus/a of the college, or if you visited the campus, or if you took some similar action. (List up to five colleges.)

College	*City/State*
_____	_____
_____	_____
_____	_____
_____	_____
_____	_____

Question 4: Thinking about the colleges that you listed or other colleges that you considered, is there one that you did not apply to for a particular reason, but that might otherwise have been one of your top choices?

YES ☐   NO ☐

If "yes," what college? (If more than one, give only the one most preferred.)
College: _____   City/State:_____

What is the main reason that you did not apply to this college?
_____

Question 5: Were you influenced to apply to certain colleges because their policies are to provide sufficient financial aid to permit any accepted student to attend?
☐ This was very important.
☐ This was somewhat important.
☐ This was not important.

Question 6: Were you influenced to apply to certain colleges because they offer scholarships to students with high academic achievement (regardless of need)?
☐ This was very important.
☐ This was somewhat important.
☐ This was not important.

Question 7: Some factors that students typically consider when choosing among colleges are listed below. Please indicate how important each of these factors is to you in choosing a college. Please circle one of the numbers for each of the factors listed below.

Factors	Degree of importance			
	Not important	Somewhat important	Important	Very important
Academic diversity (range of courses offered)	1	2	3	4
Academic facilities (library, computer resources, laboratories)	1	2	3	4
Geographical location (part of country, distance from home)	1	2	3	4
Overall academic reputation	1	2	3	4
Low overall costs (tuition, fees, room and board, other expenses)	1	2	3	4
Social climate (college atmosphere, what the student body is like, how I would fit in)	1	2	3	4
Availability of special majors, degrees, or honors programs	1	2	3	4
Community setting (urban, suburban, small town, rural)	1	2	3	4
Preparation for career or graduate and professional school opportunities	1	2	3	4
Availability of financial aid	1	2	3	4
Personal contact with college representatives (admissions staff, faculty, coaches, others)	1	2	3	4
Academic strength in your major areas of interest	1	2	3	4
Emphasis on undergraduate education (small classes, faculty contact)	1	2	3	4
Opportunities for involvement in extracurricular activities (clubs, sports, performing arts, journalism)	1	2	3	4

Question 8: In this question, we are interested in how you rate your top three college choices (that is, the colleges that you listed in Question 2). Please rate each of these colleges on the factors listed below. Circle the grade that you would assign to each college on each factor, where:

a "grade" of *A* means that you believe that the college is *excellent*
a "grade" of *B* means that you believe that the college is *good*
a "grade" of *C* means that you believe that the college is *fair*
a "grade" of *D* means that you believe that the college is *poor*
a "grade" of *F* means that you believe that the college is *unacceptable*.

Please fill in the column headings with names of the colleges you listed in Question 2. If you applied to only one or two colleges and, therefore, gave fewer than three top choices, rate only the one or two colleges to which you applied. Circle the "grade" that you would assign to each of these colleges on each of the listed factors. Even if you aren't sure, please answer in terms of your impressions of the colleges.

Factors	*First Choice* [ ]	*Second Choice* [ ]	*Third Choice* [ ]
Academic diversity (range of courses offered)	A B C D F	A B C D F	A B C D F
Academic facilities (library, computer resources, laboratories)	A B C D F	A B C D F	A B C D F

. . . . . [other factors as listed in Question 7] . . . . .

Question 9: Are there any major factors that you consider important in choosing a college that were not listed in the preceding questions? Use this space for additional comments you would like to make.

Appendix 3. The telephone interview instrument

The content and wording of the questions for the telephone interviews are described in this appendix. The actual interview form used was more complex than that presented here due to skip patterns and an elaborate format for recording admissions, financial aid, and other data for multiple colleges for each respondent. This appendix describes the interview content in an easier-to-follow format.

A "response grid" was used to record many of the answers to the repetitive questions related to the multiple colleges to which the respondents had applied. This grid was in the form of a matrix, with the rows corresponding to the colleges and the columns corresponding to the specific questions/responses of interest. The use of the grid enabled the telephone interviews to be administered in an efficient manner.

In the questionnaire below, instructions to the telephone interviewers are shown in brackets.

Screening section

Good [morning, afternoon, evening], this is _____ [your (interviewer's) name] calling for the College Board to follow up on the questionnaire you filled out for us recently.

Have you made your final decision about which college you will attend?

Yes [go to Question 1.]
No

[If "No"] When do you expect to make your final decision? _____

We'd like to talk to you after you've made your decision. We'll call back in a week or two.

What's the best time and day to reach you at home? _____

Thanks for helping us with the study. Good-bye.

Admission status by college, whether aid applied for or not

Question 1: Which college are you planning to attend?

[Record answer on response grid.]

Question 2: I'd like to check the current status of all your college applications. As I mention them, tell me if you were accepted, not accepted, put on a wait list, or have not yet heard. How about _____ [a college]?

[Read list of up to 10 colleges student reported
applying to at time of mail survey
and record admission status on grid.]

Question 3: Did you apply for financial aid at any of these colleges?

Yes
No

[If "Yes," record in grid for applicable colleges.]

Question 4: Have you applied to any other colleges?

Yes [Continue on to Question 5.]
No [Skip to Question 8.]

Question 5: Which ones?

[Record additional colleges applied to.]

Question 6: Have you heard from these colleges?

[Record admissions status for additional colleges.]

Question 7: Did you apply for financial aid at any of these colleges?

Yes
No

[If "Yes," record in grid for applicable college(s).]

Question 8: Did either of your parents attend any of the schools you applied to?

[If "Yes," record in grid for applicable college(s).]

Question 9: [Ask if accepted by more than two colleges.]
After _____ [College planning to attend], which of the schools that accepted you was your second choice?

[Record answer on grid.]

[Ask if accepted by more than three colleges.]
Which of the schools that accepted you was your third choice?

[Record answer on grid.]

Portable scholarships

Question 10: Have you been awarded any scholarships which you could use at any school you decided to attend—such as a National Merit Scholarship or one awarded by a corporation or private organization?

> Yes
>
> No   [Go to Question 14.]

[If "Yes," record source for up to five portable scholarships.]

Question 11: How much will this scholarship provide for your freshman year?

[Ask and record on portable aid grid for up to five scholarships.]

Question 12: After your first year, is there any possibility of renewing this award for your later college years?

> Definitely not
>
> Some possibility
>
> Don't know, unsure

[If "some possibility," ask Question 13.]

Question 13: Which is most accurate?

> There is only a possibility it may be renewed.
>
> You can count on it, if you maintain a required GPA.
>
> It is definitely guaranteed without any conditions.

[For each portable scholarship, record following categories on grid for renewal possibilities from response to Questions 12 and 13: "None," "Possible," "Count on it," and "Guaranteed."]

College financial aid awards

Question 14: Have you been awarded any financial aid or scholarships by any of the colleges you applied to?

> Yes
>
> No   [Skip to Question 19.]

Question 15: Which colleges offered you financial aid (and/or scholarships)?

[Record on aid grid for up to 10 colleges.]

[Questions 16, 17, and 18 are to be repeated for each college awarding the student financial aid.]

Question 16: What was the dollar value of the total financial aid package offered you by
_____ [Read each college name, one at a time]?

[Record amounts on aid grid.]

Question 17: Of that total package, how much was in the form of grants and scholarships,
how much in loans, and how much in a job?

[Record amounts on aid grid.]

Question 18: If you were to accept that financial aid package, would you expect that the
grant or scholarship portion . . .

Would definitely not be renewed in future years?
Might possibly be renewed?
Will be renewed if you maintain a required GPA?
Is definitely guaranteed without conditions?

[Record renewability response (1, 2, 3, 4) on aid grid.]

Factors in college choice

Question 19: On the questionnaire you returned, you told us how important certain factors
were to you in choosing a college. I'd like to ask you how you feel about a
few of these factors, now that you have actually made a decision.

As I read each one, please give me an answer from 1 to 4, where 1 means
the factor was "not important," 2 means it was "somewhat important," 3
means it was "important," and 4 means it was "very important" to you in
making your final decision.

[Respondents randomly assigned to Form A or Form B.]

Form A

For example, how important was . . . [use random start]
—Academic diversity (range of courses offered)?
—Geographical location (part of the country, distance from home)?
—Low overall costs (tuition, fees, room and board, other expenses)?
—Availability of special majors, degrees or honors programs?
—Preparation for career or graduate and professional school opportunities?
—Personal contact with college representatives (admissions staff, faculty,
coaches, others)?
—Emphasis on undergraduate education (small classes, faculty contact,
etc.)?

Form B

For example, how important was . . . [use random start]
—Academic facilities (library, computer resources, laboratories, etc.)?
—Overall academic reputation?
—Social climate (college atmosphere, what the student body is like, how I would fit in)?
—Community setting (urban, suburban, small town, rural)?
—Availability of financial aid?
—Academic strength in your major areas of interest?
—Opportunities for involvement in extracurricular activities (clubs, sports, performing arts, etc.)?

[Repeat Question 20 for each of the seven choice factors rated in Question 19.]

Question 20: Now, thinking about _____ [a choice factor from question 19], using the grades A for "Excellent," B for "Good," C for "Fair," D for "Poor," and F for "Unacceptable," how would you grade _____ [initial first-choice college] on _____ [choice factor]?

And how would you grade _____ [initial second-choice college] on this factor?

How about _____ [initial third-choice college]?

[Record responses on grid.]

Contacts with colleges

Question 21: Before you made your final college choice, did you have any contact with any of the colleges which accepted you, after the initial acceptance letter? For example, did you receive any personal letters from staff members or alumni?

Yes
No   [Skip to Question 24.]

Question 22: Which [staff members, alumni] from which schools wrote you letters?

[Record on grid for each applicable college
by each type of person contacting:
President/Dean
Faculty
Coach
Student
Alumni

Admissions officer
Honors program
Other]

Question 23: Did any of these letters have a particularly positive or negative influence on your decision about where to go to school?

[If "Yes"] Which letters had an influence?

[Circle + or − on response grid.]

Question 24: Have any college staff members or alumni called you since you received your acceptance letter?

Yes
No [Skip to Question 27.]

Question 25: Which [staff members, alumni] from which schools called you?

[Record on grid for each applicable college
by each type of person contacting:
President/Dean
Faculty
Coach
Student
Alumni
Admissions officer
Honors program
Other]

Question 26: Did any of these calls have a particularly positive or negative influence on your decision about where to go to school?

[If "Yes"] Which calls had an influence?

[Circle + or − on response grid.]

Question 27: Did you meet with any college staff members or alumni after you were accepted?

Yes
No [Skip to Question 30.]

Question 28: Which [staff members, alumni] from which schools met with you?

[Record on grid for each applicable college
by each type of person contacting:
President/Dean
Faculty

Coach
Student
Alumni
Admissions officer
Honors program
Other]

Question 29: Did any of these meetings have a particularly positive or negative influence on your decision about where to go to school?

[If "Yes"] Which meetings had an influence?

[Circle + or − on response grid.]

Question 30: Did you receive any additional descriptive literature about any of the colleges which accepted you?

Yes

No [Skip to Question 32.]

Question 31: Which colleges sent you descriptive literature?

[Record on grid.]

Question 32: Did you attend any parties for accepted candidates sponsored by alumni or other college representatives?

Yes

No [Skip to Question 34.]

Question 33: Which colleges sponsored parties which you attended?

[Record on grid.]

Question 34: Have you visited the campuses of any of the colleges which accepted you— either before or after you were accepted?

Yes

No [Skip to Question 36.]

Question 35: Which colleges did you visit?

[Record on grid.]

Question 36: Did any of these activities (receiving literature, attending parties, or visiting campuses) have a particularly positive or negative influence on your decision about where to go to school?

[If "Yes"] Which activities had an influence?

[Circle + or − on response grid.]

Academic bases for scholarships

Question 37: [Ask only if respondent was offered scholarship by any college.] Was all or any part of the scholarship(s) you were offered by any college awarded for your academic performance?

> Yes
> No [Skip to Question 44.]

Question 38: Which colleges offered you scholarships based on your academic qualifications?

> [Record on grid.]

Question 39: For the academic scholarship offered you by _____ were you required to submit any special application or other written materials or have an interview specifically related to the scholarship award?

> [Record "Yes" = 1, "No" = 2 on grid.]

Question 40: Were you invited to any type of on-campus ceremony to receive your scholarship from _____ which involved an overnight or weekend stay?

> [Record "Yes" = 1, "No" = 2 on grid.]

Question 41: Did you receive any of the following relating to this scholarship (or would you have received them if you had accepted the award): an award or plaque; an invitation to a special reception or dinner in your home area; any special recognition planned for your high school graduation; or any other symbolic recognition of achievement?

> [Record "Yes" = 1, "No" = 2 on grid.]

Question 42: If you [accept, had accepted] this scholarship, [will, would] you be part of any honors program or special group next year at college, along with other scholarship winners?

> [Record "Yes" = 1, "No" = 2 on grid.]

Question 43: [Ask if respondent answered "Yes" to any questions 39–42.] Did any of these requirements, honors, or special events have a significant positive or negative influence on your decision about where to go to college?

[If "Yes"] Which events, what influence?

> [Circle + or − on response grid.]

Self-reports on change in college choice

Question 44: [Ask if respondent is not going to attend the top college (Highest prior-preference college) to which he or she was admitted.]

In the mail questionnaire you sent us, you indicated that _____ [top admitted school] was one of your top choices. What was the one main reason you chose to go to a different school?

[Record up to three reasons.]

Question 45: [Ask if respondent was admitted to more than one college.] Think about the school you decided to attend and your second-choice school. Suppose your second-choice school offered you an extra $500 scholarship. Would that have changed your decision?

How about if they offered an extra $1,000?

How about an extra $2,000?

How about an extra $3,000?

[Record 1 = "Yes," 2 = "No" on response grid.]

[If "Yes" to any of these questions, skip to closing section.]

Closing Section

Thank you for your cooperation in the study. That's all the questions we have for you.

Appendix 4. An illustrative choice probability calculation

In this appendix, we illustrate the use of the multinomial logit model and our estimates of its parameters (relative importances of the variables) in calculating choice probabilities in various sample situations. These situations/examples/scenarios are described in the latter part of Chapter 4.

Consider the situation below:

Choice set composition	Three colleges, denoted as colleges A, B, and C. (College A will be constructed to be an average college, B will be a public institution, and C will be an average top-seven school.)
Prior preference situation	Colleges A, B, and C are the first, second, and third prior preference alternatives, respectively.
Financial considerations	The COSTS, GRANTAID, and OTHERAID situations are as follows:

	COSTS	GRANTAID	OTHERAID
College A	$10,500	$1,240	$ 500
College B	$ 5,500	$ 0	$ 0
College C	$14,000	$3,000	$2,000

College-specific considerations	Colleges A and B are not top-seven schools; College C is an average top-seven institution.
Other relevant factors	The mean SAT scores of students at colleges A, B, and C are 550, 500, and 600, respectively. Assume that the student has an SAT score of 675. Perceived renewability of the financial aid is "probable" at college A (RENEWAL = 3, RENEWM = 0) and "possible" at college C (RENEWAL = 2, RENEWM = 0). Renewability of aid is not relevant at college B (RENEWAL = 0, RENEWM = 1), since no aid was offered in the first instance.

Table A4.1. Details of the illustrative choice probability calculation

	Weight[1]	College A Value of variable	College A Partial utility score[2]	College B Value of variable	College B Partial utility score	College C Value of variable	College C Partial utility score
FIRST	3.2762	1.000	3.2762	0.000	0.0000	0.000	0.0000
SECOND	1.9061	0.000	0.0000	1.000	1.9061	0.000	0.0000
THIRD	1.3063	0.000	0.0000	0.000	0.0000	1.000	1.3063
COSTS	−0.1313	10.500	−1.3786	5.500	−0.7221	14.000	−1.8382
COSTSM	−0.0400	0.000	0.0000	0.000	0.0000	0.000	0.0000
TOTALAID	0.0770	0.000	0.0000	0.000	0.0000	0.000	0.0000
GRANTAID	0.2907	1.240	0.3605	0.000	0.0000	3.000	0.8721
OTHERAID	0.0158	0.500	0.0079	0.000	0.0000	2.000	0.0316
RENEWAL	0.3062	3.000	0.9186	0.000	0.0000	2.000	0.6124
RENEWM	0.6075	0.000	0.0000	1.000	0.6075	0.000	0.0000
SATFIT	−0.0041	125.000	−0.5125	175.000	−0.7175	75.000	−0.3075
SATM	0.0631	0.000	0.0000	0.000	0.0000	0.000	0.0000
COLLEGE[3]	1.1546	0.000	0.0000	0.000	0.0000	1.000	1.1546
Total utility score[4]			2.6721		1.0740		1.8313
Adjusted utility score[5]			14.4703		2.9271		6.2420
Probability of choice[6]			0.6121		0.1238		0.2641

1. With the exception of the variable COLLEGE, the "Weight" values are the coefficient estimates of the multinomial logit model. They are taken directly from the results reported in Table 4.9. The weights are the estimated values of the θ parameters in equation (A2) in Appendix 1.

2. "Partial utility score" is the product of the weight and the "Value of variable." The partial utility scores are the individual terms $\theta_k Z_{ijk}$ in equation (A2) in Appendix 1.

3. "COLLEGE" refers to an average top-seven college; its weight is the mean college-specific coefficient estimate for the top-seven colleges as reported in Table 4.9.

4. "Total utility score" is equal to the sum of all the partial-utility-score values for a college alternative. Total utility score is the V_{ij} term in equations (A1) and (A2) in Appendix 1.

5. "Adjusted utility score" equals the exponential of total utility score. For example, the adjusted utility score of college A is equal to exp(2.6721) = 14.4703.

6. The "probability of choice" for an alternative is equal to its adjusted utility score divided by the sum of all the adjusted utility scores of the college alternatives in the choice set. For example, the probability of choice of college A is equal to 0.6121 = (14.4703/(14.4703 + 2.9271 + 6.2420)). See equation (A1) in Appendix 1.

The details of the choice-probability calculations are shown in Table A4.1. As may be noted, the estimated choice probabilities for colleges A, B, and C are approximately 0.61 (61 percent), 0.12 (12 percent), and 0.27 (27 percent), respectively.

In this situation, note that being first choice on a prior preference basis propels college A well ahead of the others. The considerable advantage that college B has over college C due to being the second choice on a prior preference basis is offset by B's much poorer SATFIT and the scholarship aid offered by college C. Also, the top-seven effect has a considerable impact on the choice probability for college C.

References

Anderson, Norman H. 1974. "Information Integration Theory: A Brief Survey," in D. H. Krantz, R. C. Atkinson, R. D. Luce, and P. Suppes (eds.), *Contemporary Developments in Mathematical Psychology*, Volume 2. San Francisco: Freeman, pp. 236–305.

———. 1981. *Foundations of Information Integration Theory*. New York: Academic.

———. 1982. *Methods of Information Integration Theory*. New York: Academic.

Astin, Alexander W., Kenneth C. Green, William S. Korn, and Mary Jane Maier. 1983. *The American Freshman: National Norms For Fall 1983*. Los Angeles: American Council on Education and the Cooperative Institutional Research Program, The Higher Education Research Institute, University of California at Los Angeles.

———. 1984. *The American Freshman: National Norms For Fall 1984*. Los Angeles: American Council on Education and the Cooperative Institutional Research Program, The Higher Education Research Institute, University of California at Los Angeles

———. 1985. *The American Freshman: National Norms For Fall 1985*. Los Angeles: American Council on Education and the Cooperative Institutional Research Program, The Higher Education Research Institute, University of California at Los Angeles.

Barron's. 1980. *Barron's Profiles of American Colleges—Volume 1: Descriptions of the Colleges*, Twelfth Edition. Woodbury, New York: Barron's Educational Services.

Ben-Akiva, Moshe, and Steven R. Lerman. 1985. *Discrete Choice Analysis: Theory and Application to Travel Demand*. Cambridge, Mass.: MIT Press.

Brunswik, E. 1952. *The Conceptual Framework of Psychology*. Chicago: University of Chicago Press.

Chapman, Randall G. 1977. "Buyer Behavior in Higher Education: An Analysis of College Choice Decision Making," Ph.D. diss., Graduate School of Industrial Administration, Carnegie-Mellon University.

———1979. "Pricing Policy and the College Choice Process," *Research in Higher Education*, 10 (1):37 57.

Chapman, Randall G., and Richard Staelin. 1982. "Exploiting Rank Ordered Choice Set Data Within the Stochastic Utility Model," *Journal of Marketing Research*, 19 (August):288–301.

College Board and American Association of Collegiate Registrars and Admissions Officers. 1980. *Undergraduate Admissions: The Realities of Institutional Policies, Practices, and Procedures*. New York: College Entrance Examination Board.

College Board. 1984. *Annual Survey of Colleges 1984–85: Summary Statistics*. New York: College Entrance Examination Board.

College Board. 1984. *The College Handbook 1984–85*, Twenty-second Edition. New York: College Entrance Examination Board.

College Board and National Association of Student Financial Aid Administrators. 1984. "A Survey of Undergraduate Need Analysis Policies, Practices, and Procedures." Mimeo., College Entrance Examination Board, New York.

Dillon, William R., Donald G. Frederick, and Vanchai Tangpanichdee. 1985. "Decision Issues in Building Perceptual Product Spaces With Multi-Attribute Rating Data." *Journal of Consumer Research* 12 (June):47–63.

Fiske, Edward B. 1982. *Selective Guide to Colleges*. New York: Times Books.

Gensch, Dennis H., and Wilfred W. Recker. 1979.

"The Multinomial, Multiattribute Logit Choice Model." *Journal of Marketing Research* 16(February):124–132.

Hauser, John R., Alice M. Tybout, and Frank S. Koppelman. 1981. "Consumer-Oriented Transportation Service Planning: Consumer Analysis and Strategies." In Randall L. Schultz (ed.), *Applications of Management Science: Volume 1:* 91–138. New York: JAI Press.

Hensher, David A., and Lester W. Johnson. 1981. *Applied Discrete-Choice Modeling*. London: Croom Helm.

Huff, Robert. 1975. "No-Need Scholarships." *The College Board Review* 95(Spring):13–15.

Kohn, Meir G., Charles F. Manski, and David Mundel. 1976. "An Empirical Investigation of Factors Influencing College-Going Behavior." *Annals of Economic and Social Measurement* 5(Fall):391–419.

Litten, Larry H., Daniel Sullivan, and David L. Brodigan. 1983. *Applying Marketing Research in College Admissions*. New York: College Entrance Examination Board.

McClintock, John. 1982. *100 Top Colleges: How to Choose and Get In*. New York: John Wiley.

McFadden, Daniel. 1974. "Conditional Logit Analysis of Qualitative Choice Behavior." In Paul Zarembka (ed.), *Frontiers in Econometrics:*105–42. New York: Academic.

Maddala, G. S. 1983. *Limited-Dependent and Qualitative Variables in Econometrics*. New York: Cambridge University Press.

Manski, Charles F., and David A. Wise. 1983. *College Choice in America*. Cambridge, Mass.: Harvard University Press.

Porter, Betsy A., and Suzanne K. McColloch. 1982. "The Use of No-Need Academic Scholarships in U.S. Universities and Colleges: A Survey." Mimeo.

Punj, Girish N., and Richard Staelin. 1978. "The Choice Process For Graduate Business Schools." *Journal of Marketing Research* 15(November):588–98.

Radner, Roy, and Leonard S. Miller. 1975. *Demand and Supply in U.S. Higher Education*. New York: McGraw-Hill.

Sidar, Alexander G., and David A. Potter. 1978. *No-Need/Merit Awards: A Survey of Their Use at Four-Year Public and Private Colleges and Universities*. New York: College Entrance Examination Board.

Tybout, Alice M., and John R. Hauser. 1981. "A Marketing Audit Using a Conceptual Model of Consumer Behavior: Application and Evaluation." *Journal of Marketing* 45(Summer):82–101.

Urban, Glen L., and John R. Hauser. 1980. *Design and Marketing of New Products*. Englewood Cliffs, New Jersey: Prentice-Hall.

Venti, Stephen F. 1983. "The Allocation of Discretionary Grant Aid." In Charles F. Manski and David A. Wise, *College Choice in America*. Cambridge, Mass.: Harvard University Press, pp. 91–104.

Wald, A. 1943. "Tests of Statistical Hypotheses Concerning Several Parameters When the Number of Observations Is Large." *Transactions of the American Mathematical Society* 54:426–82.

Watson, Peter L., and Richard B. Westin. 1975. "Transferability of Disaggregated Model Choice Models." *Regional Science and Urban Economics* 5(May):227–49.